EASY GUITAR
WITH NOTES & TAB

CHART HITS
OF 2021-2022

T0071616

ISBN 978-1-70516-066-4

Hal•Leonard®

Visit Hal Leonard Online at
www.halleonard.com

World headquarters, contact:
Hal Leonard
7777 West Bluemound Road
Milwaukee, WI 53213
Email: info@halleonard.com

In Europe, contact:
Hal Leonard Europe Limited
42 Wigmore Street
Marylebone, London, W1U 2RN
Email: info@halleonardeurope.com

In Australia, contact:
Hal Leonard Australia Pty. Ltd.
4 Lentara Court
Cheltenham, Victoria, 3192 Australia
Email: info@halleonard.com.au

STRUM AND PICK PATTERNS

This chart contains the suggested strum and pick patterns that are referred to by number at the beginning of each song in this book. The symbols ⊓ and ∨ in the strum patterns refer to down and up strokes, respectively. The letters in the pick patterns indicate which right-hand fingers play which strings.

p = thumb
i = index finger
m = middle finger
a = ring finger

For example; Pick Pattern 2
is played: thumb - index - middle - ring

Strum Patterns   ## Pick Patterns

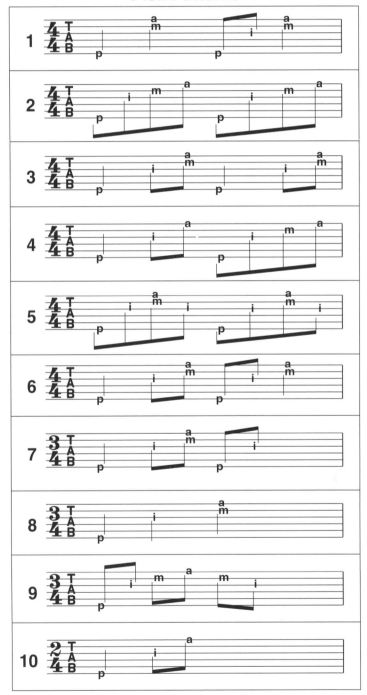

You can use the 3/4 Strum and Pick Patterns in songs written in compound meter (6/8, 9/8, 12/8, etc.).
For example, you can accompany a song in 6/8 by playing the 3/4 pattern twice in each measure.
The 4/4 Strum and Pick Patterns can be used for songs written in cut time (¢) by doubling the note
time values in the patterns. Each pattern would therefore last two measures in cut time.

Brightside

Words and Music by Jeremy Fraites and Wesley Schultz

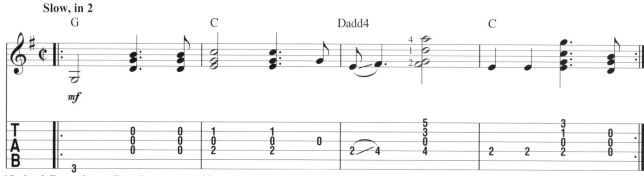

*Capo III

Strum Pattern: 3
Pick Pattern: 3

Intro
Slow, in 2

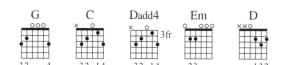

*Optional: To match recording, place capo at 3rd fret.

Verse

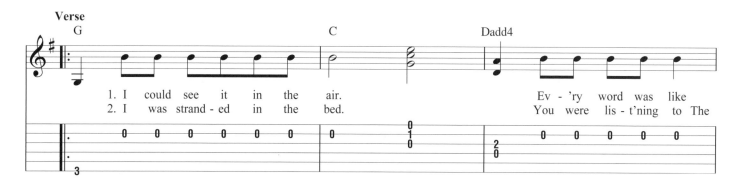

1. I could see it in the air.
2. I was strand-ed in the bed.

Ev - 'ry word was like
You were lis - t'ning to The

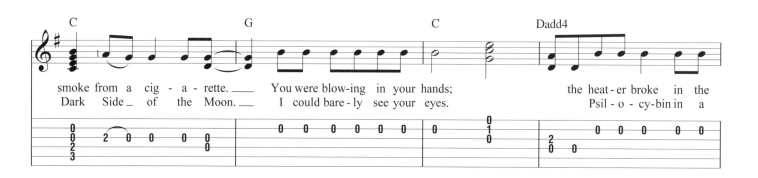

smoke from a cig - a - rette. ___ You were blow-ing in your hands;
Dark Side ___ of the Moon. ___ I could bare-ly see your eyes.

the heat - er broke in the
Psil - o - cy-bin in a

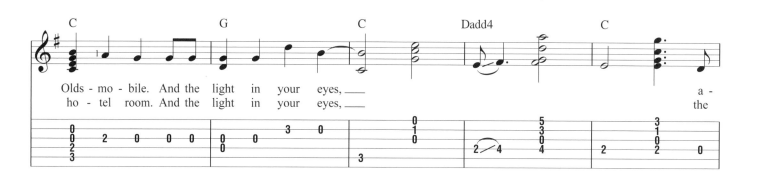

Olds - mo - bile. And the light in your eyes, ___
ho - tel room. And the light in your eyes, ___

a -
the

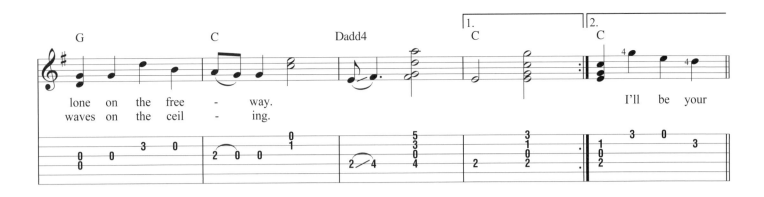

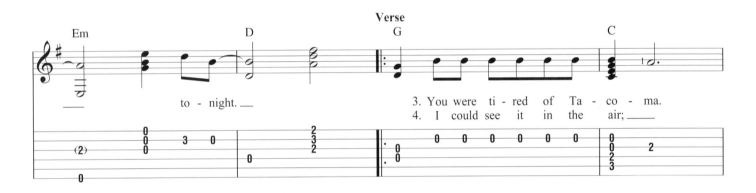

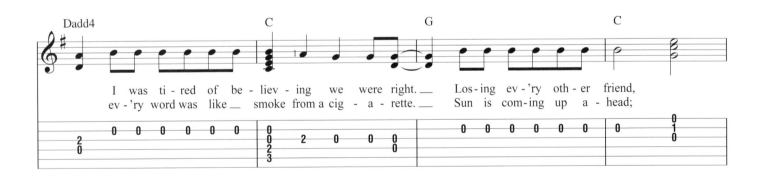

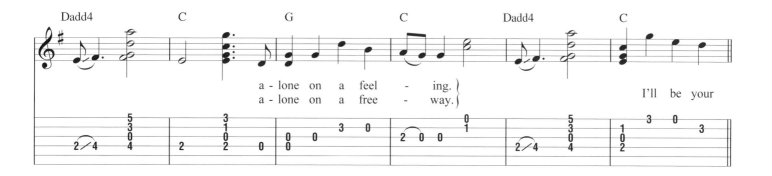

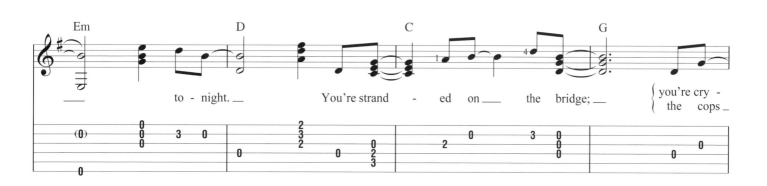

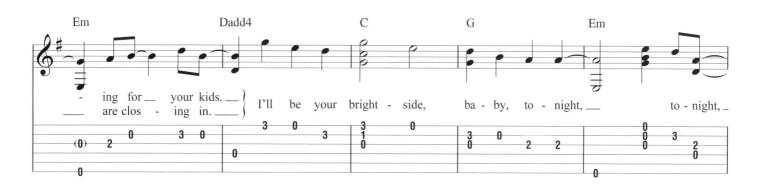

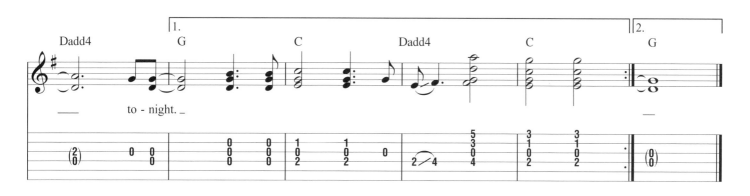

All Too Well

Words and Music by Taylor Swift and Liz Rose

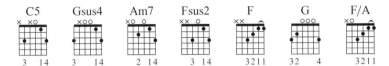

Strum Pattern: 1
Pick Pattern: 4

*Let chord ring.

Interlude

2. Oh, your

𝄋 Verse

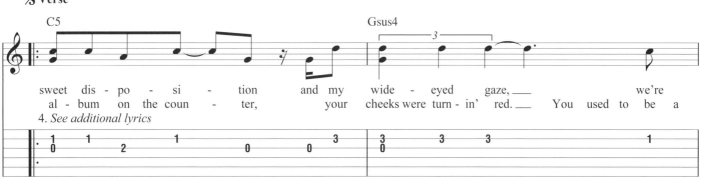

sweet dis-po-si-tion and my wide-eyed gaze,___ we're
al-bum on the coun-ter, your cheeks were turn-in' red.___ You used to be a
4. See additional lyrics

sing-in' in the car ___ get-tin' lost ___ up-state. Au-tumn leaves ___ fall-in' down like
lit-tle kid with glass-es in a twin-size bed. ___ And your moth-er's tell-in' sto-ries 'bout you on the

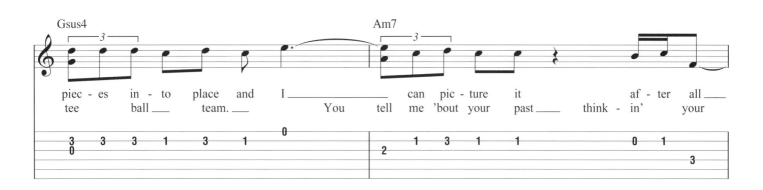

piec-es in-to place and I_____ can pic-ture it af-ter all___
tee ball ___ team. ___ You tell me 'bout your past ___ think-in' your

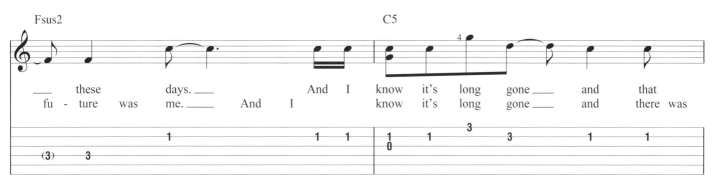

___ these days. ___ And I know it's long gone ___ and that
fu-ture was me. ___ And I know it's long gone ___ and there was

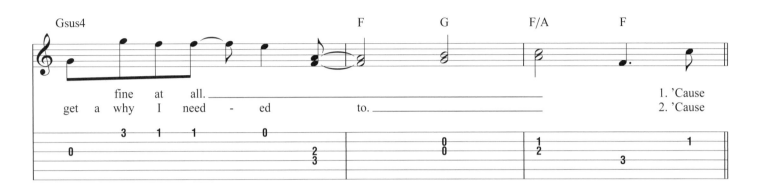

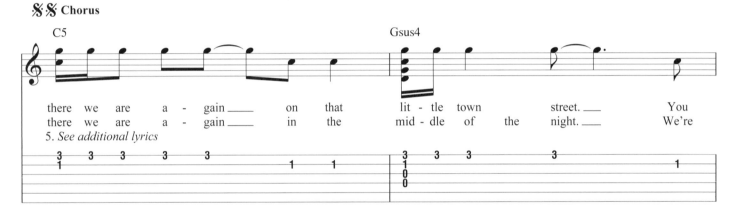

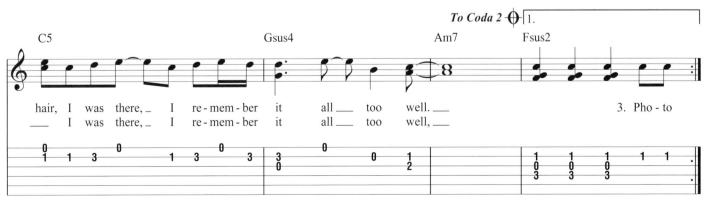

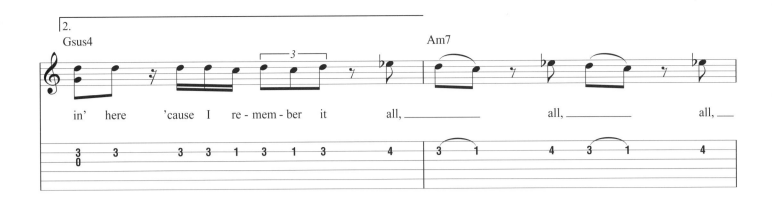

D.S. al Coda 1

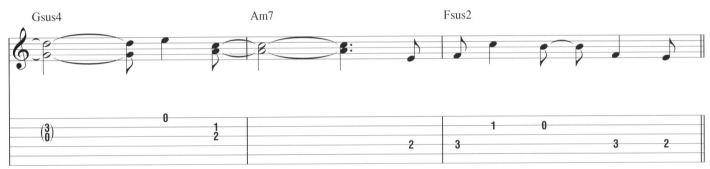

✛ **Coda 1**

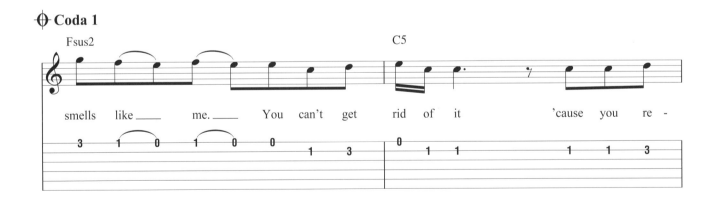

D.S.S. al Coda 2

Coda 2

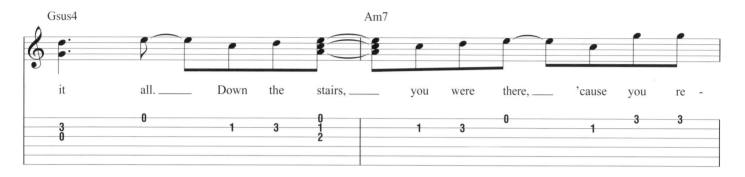

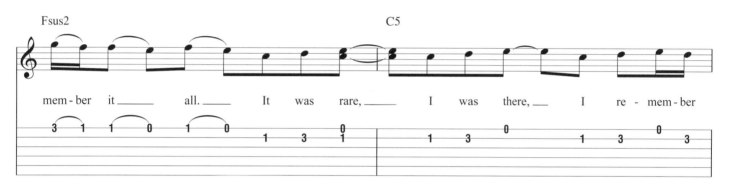

Additional Lyrics

4. Time won't fly, it's like I'm paralyzed by it.
   I'd like to be my old self again, but I'm still try'n' to find it.
   After plaid shirt days and nights when you made me your own,
   Now you mail back my things and I walk home alone.
   But you keep my old scarf from that very first week
   'Cause it reminds you of innocence and it smells like me.
   You can't get rid of it
   'Cause you remember it all too well, yeah.

Chorus 5. 'Cause there we are again when I loved you so
   Back before you lost the one real thing you've ever known.
   It was rare, I was there, I remember it all too well.
   Wind in my hair, you were there, you remember it all.
   Down the stairs, you were there, 'cause you remember it all.
   It was rare, I was there, I remember it all too well.

Buy Dirt

Words and Music by Jordan Davis, Jacob Davis, Joshua Jenkins and Matt Jenkins

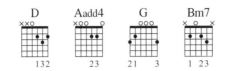

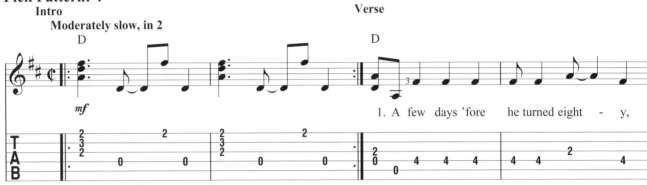

*Capo II

Strum Pattern: 6
Pick Pattern: 4

Intro

Moderately slow, in 2

Verse

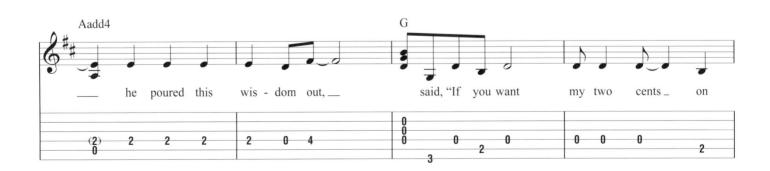

*Optional: To match recording, place capo at 2nd fret.

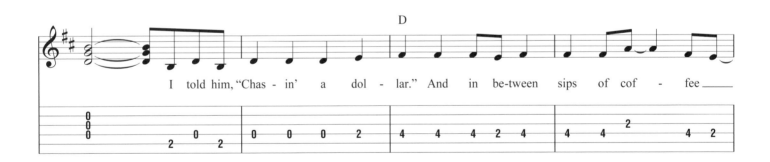

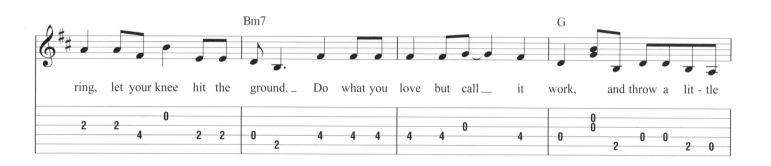

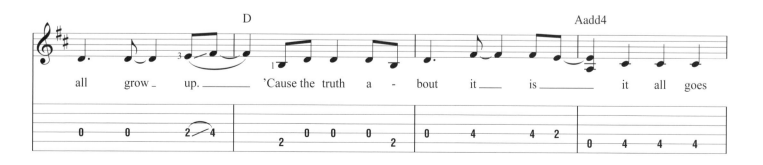

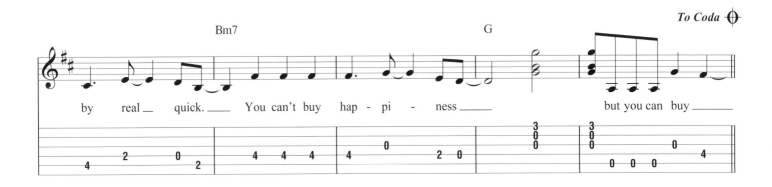

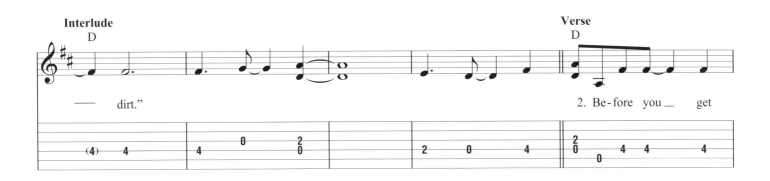

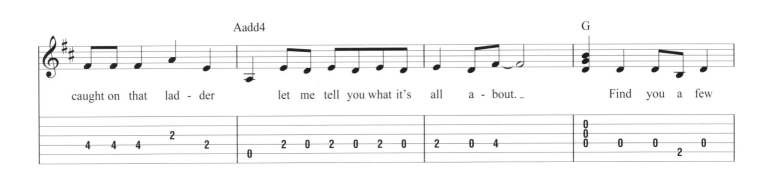

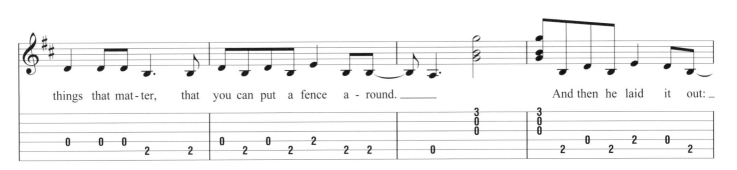

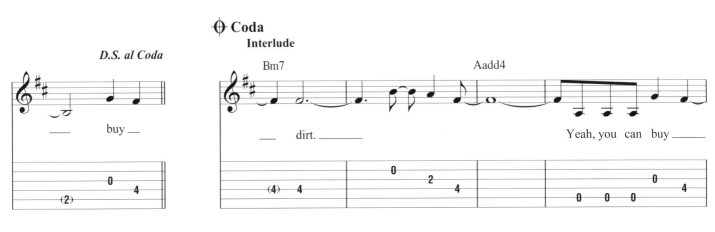

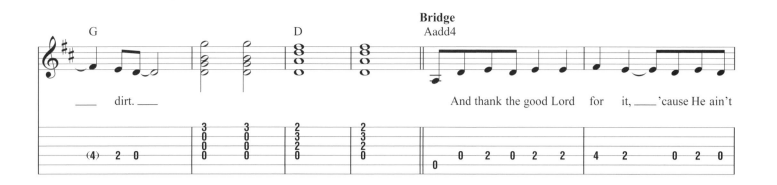

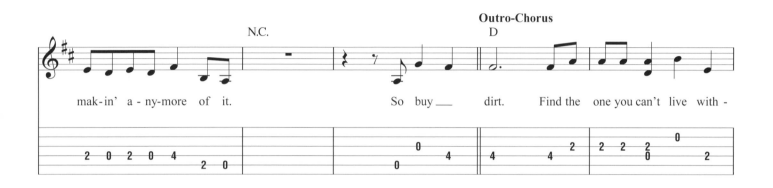

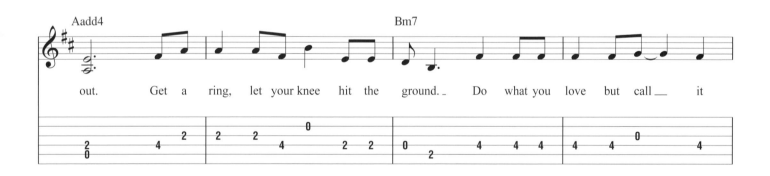

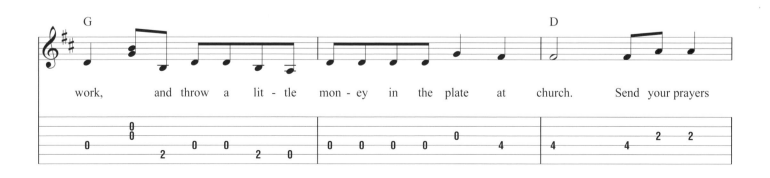

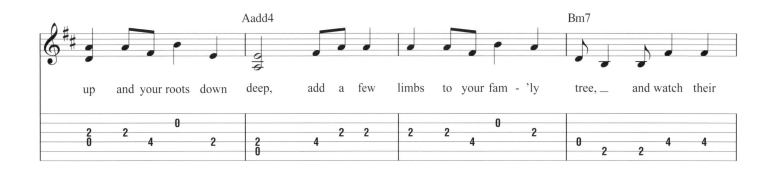

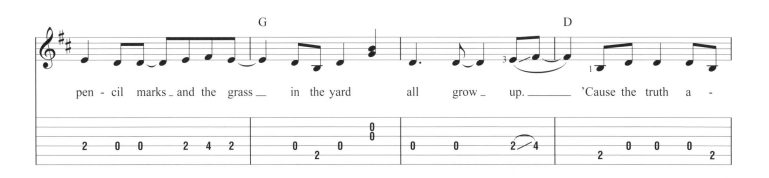

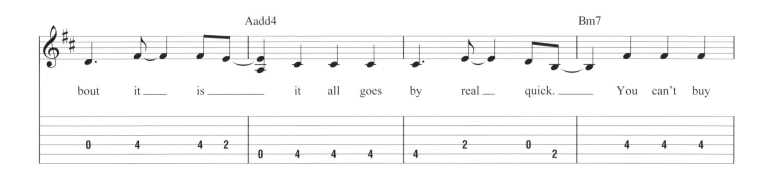

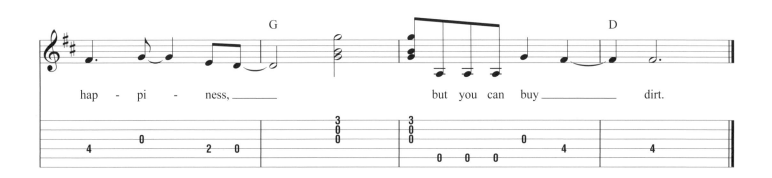

Easy on Me

Words and Music by Adele Adkins and Greg Kurstin

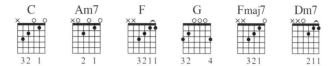

*Capo V

Strum Pattern: 3, 4

Pick Pattern: 3, 4

Intro

Moderately slow, in 2

*Optional: To match recording, place capo at 5th fret.

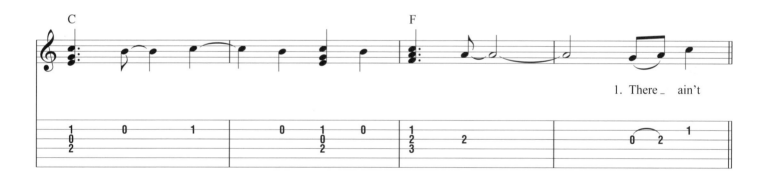

1. There ___ ain't

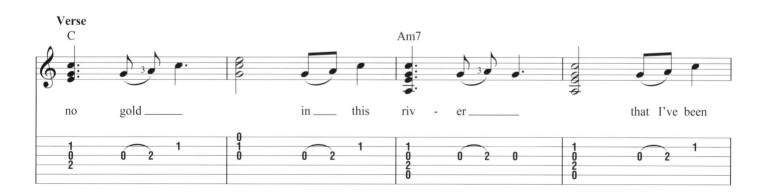

no gold _____ in ___ this riv - er _____ that I've been

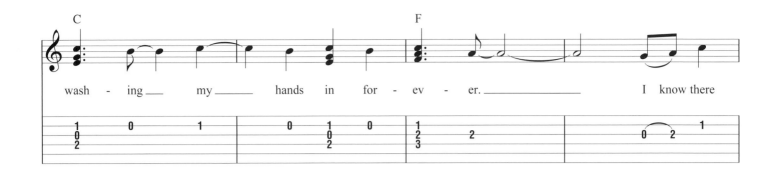

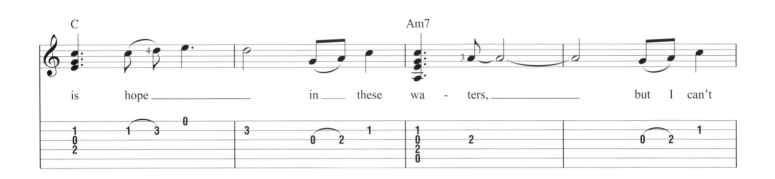

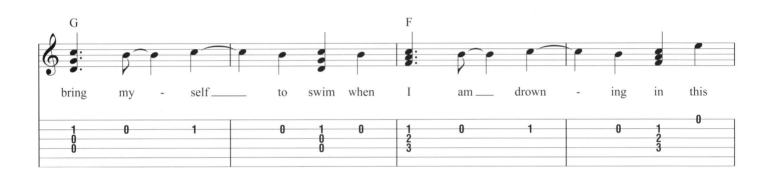

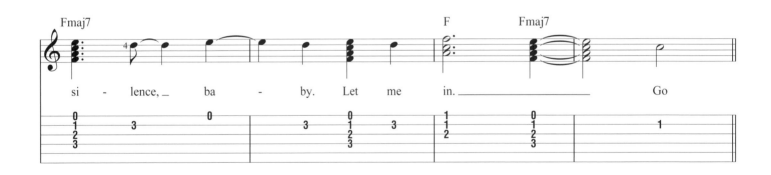

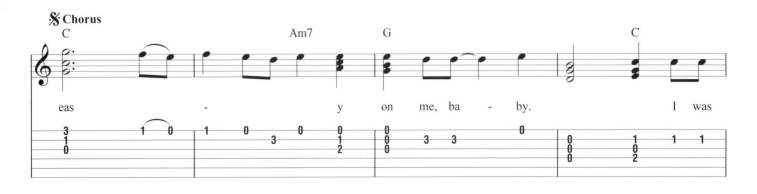

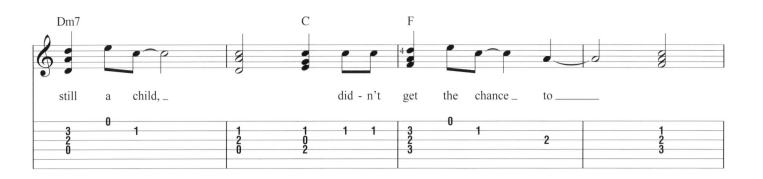

still a child, _ did - n't get the chance _ to _____

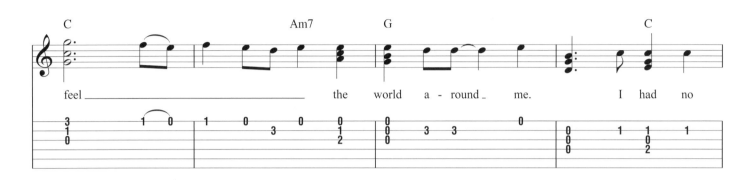

feel _____ the world a - round _ me. I had no

To Coda 1 🜉
To Coda 2 🜉

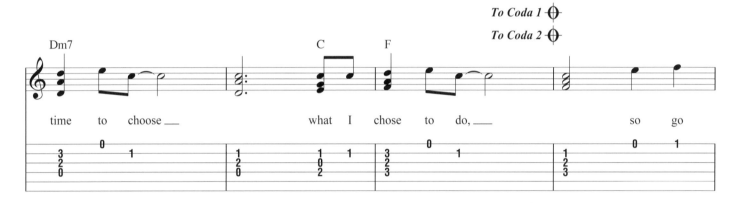

time to choose ___ what I chose to do, ___ so go

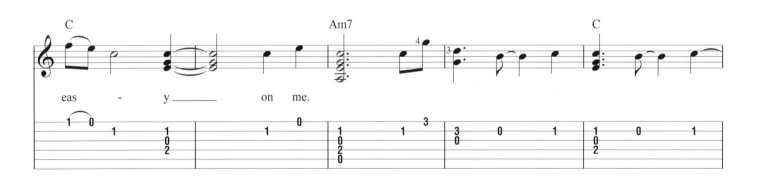

eas - y ___ on me.

Verse

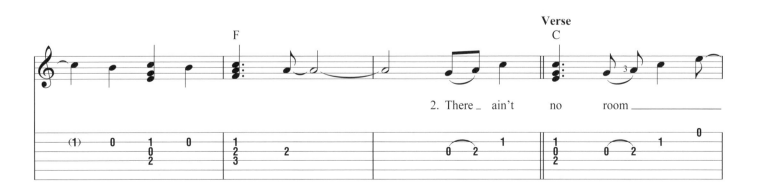

2. There _ ain't no room _____

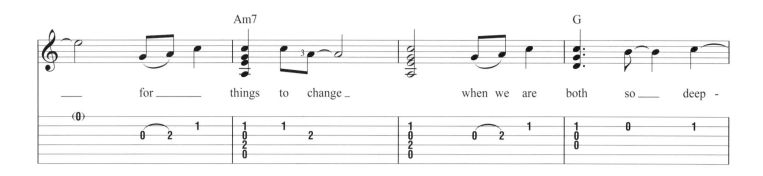

for _____ things to change _____ when we are both so _____ deep-

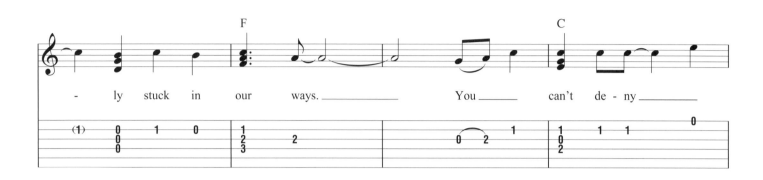

-ly stuck in our ways. _____ You _____ can't de-ny _____

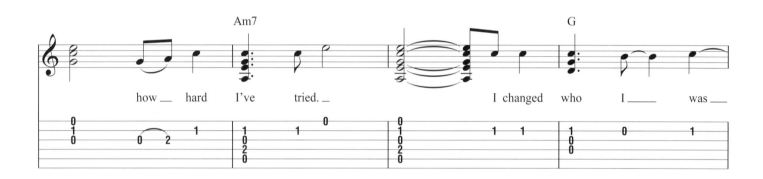

how _____ hard I've tried. _____ I changed who I _____ was _____

D.S. al Coda 1

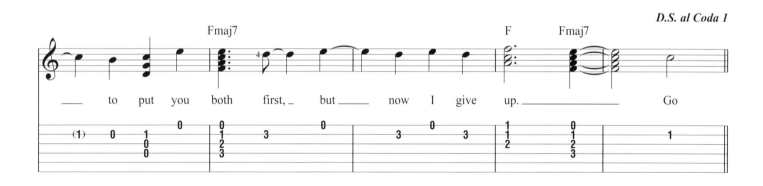

_____ to put you both first, _ but _____ now I give up. _____ Go

$\oplus$ **Coda 1**

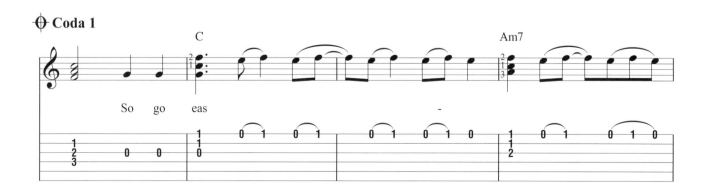

So go eas

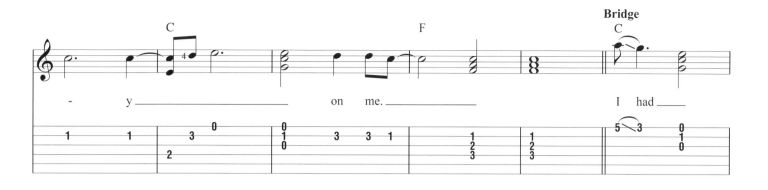

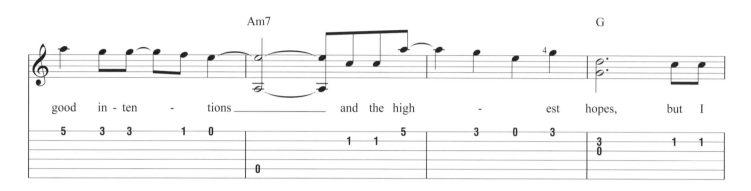

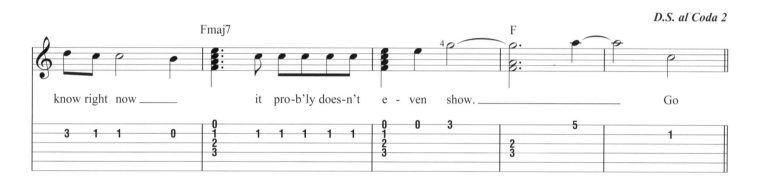

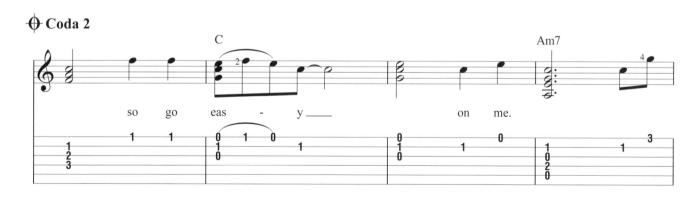

Fancy Like

Words and Music by Walker Hayes, Josh Jenkins, Shane Stevens and Cameron Bartolini

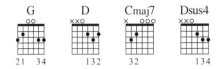

*Tune down 1/2 step:
(low to high) E♭-A♭-D♭-G♭-B♭-E♭

Strum Pattern: 5
Pick Pattern: 4

Intro
Moderately slow, in 2

*Optional: To match recording, tune down 1/2 step.

1. My girl is

Verse

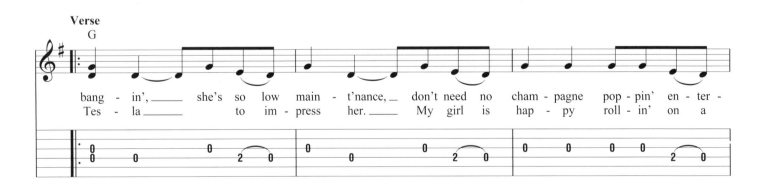

bang - in',____ she's so low main - t'nance, don't need no cham - pagne pop - pin' en - ter -
Tes - la ____ to im - press her. ___ My girl is hap - py roll - in' on a

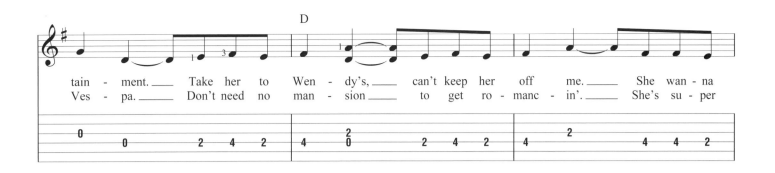

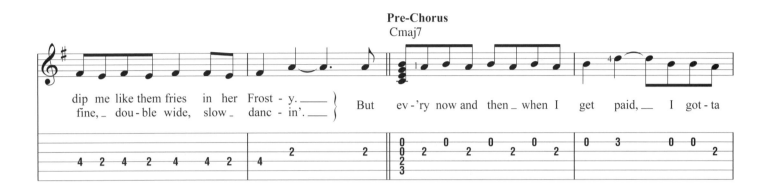

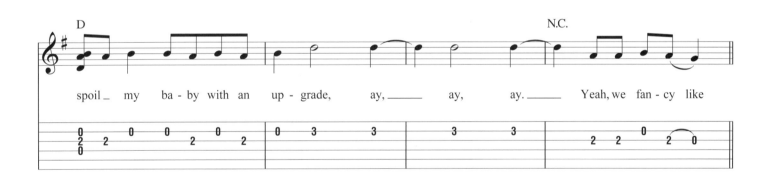

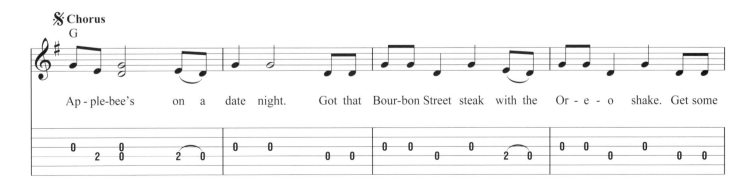

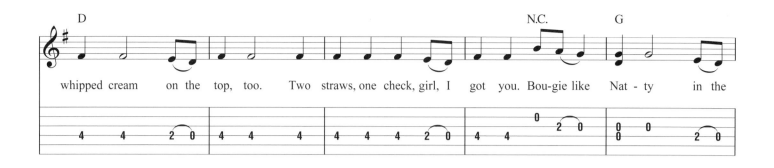

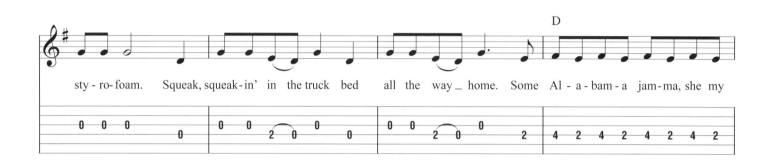

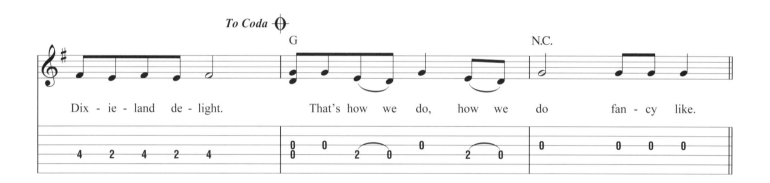

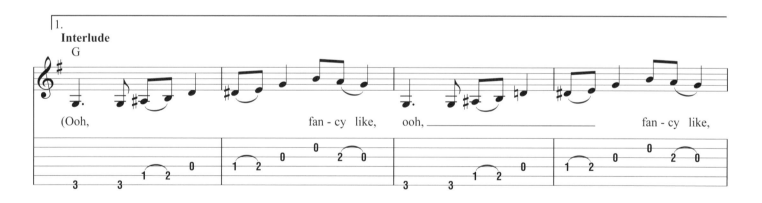

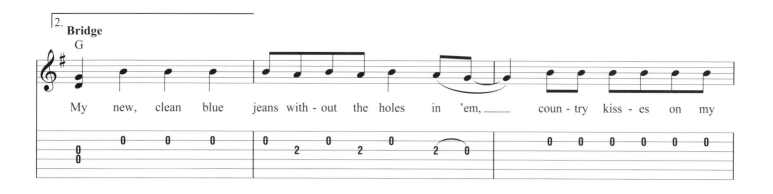

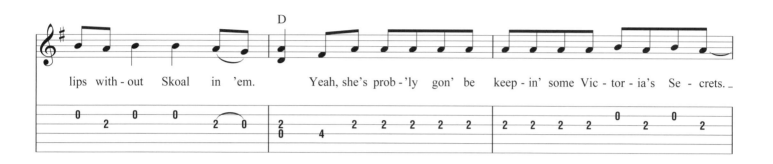

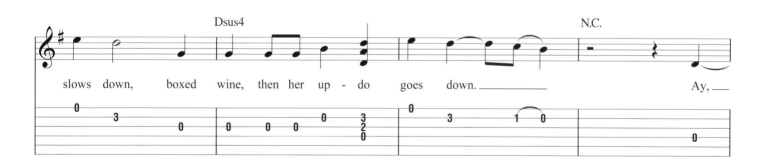

Coda

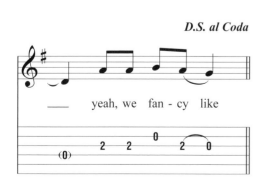

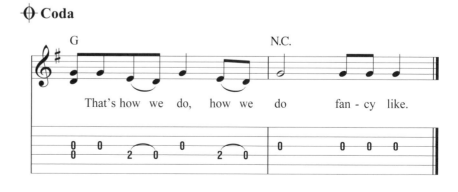

25

Follow You

Words and Music by Dan Reynolds, Wayne Sermon, Ben McKee,
Daniel Platzman, Elley Duhé, Joel Little and Fransisca Hall

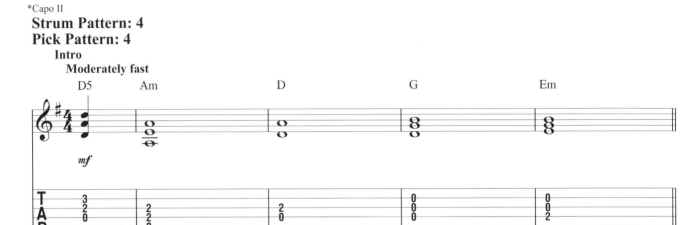

*Capo II

Strum Pattern: 4
Pick Pattern: 4

Intro
Moderately fast

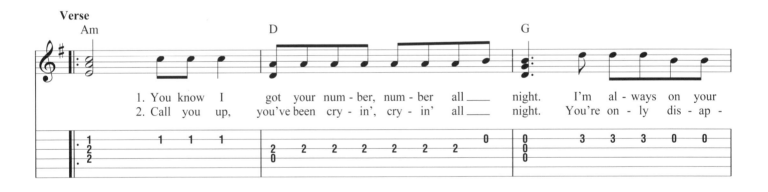

*Optional: To match recording, place capo at 2nd fret.

Verse

1. You know I got your num - ber, num - ber all ___ night. I'm al - ways on your
2. Call you up, you've been cry - in', cry - in' all ___ night. You're on - ly dis - ap -

team, I got your back, al - right. Tak - in' those, tak - in' those loss - es if it treats you ___
point - ed in your - self, al - right. Tak - in' those, tak - in' those loss - es if it treats you ___

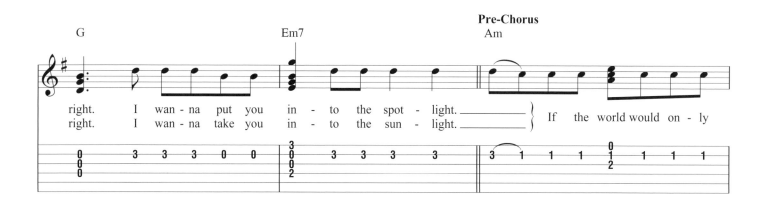

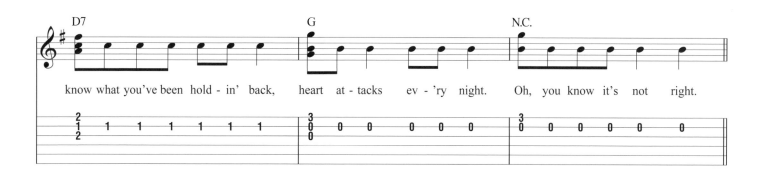

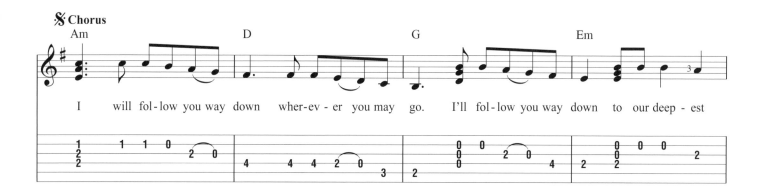

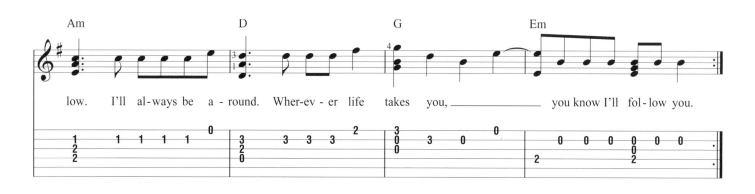

Interlude

Oo.__ La, da, da, da, da, da. La, da, da, da, da, da. La, da, da, da, da, da. You know I'll fol-low you.

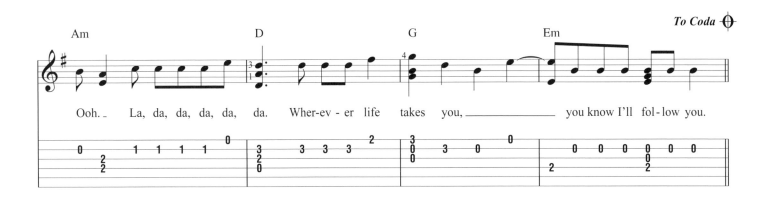

To Coda ⊕

Ooh.__ La, da, da, da, da, da. Wher-ev-er life takes you,_____ you know I'll fol-low you.

Bridge

Ooh.__ She's not the type to give her-self e-nough love.___ She live her life, hand in a tight glove.__

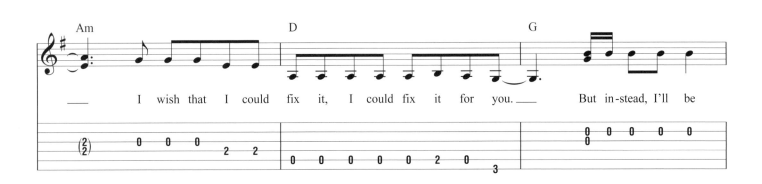

___ I wish that I could fix it, I could fix it for you.___ But in-stead, I'll be

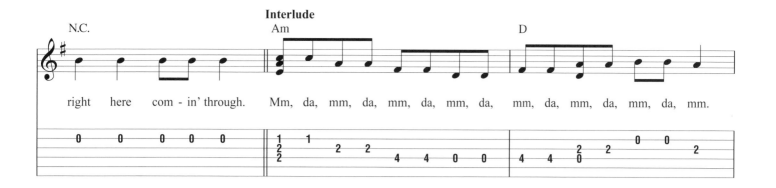

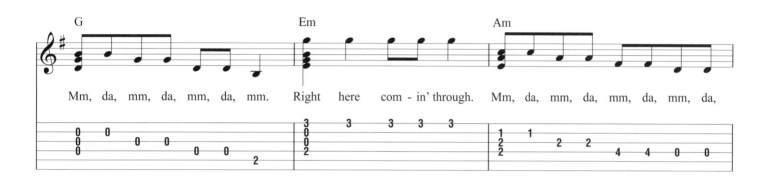

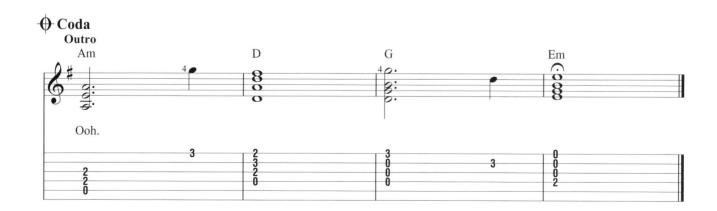

Ghost

Words and Music by Justin Bieber, Jonathan Bellion,
Jordan Johnson, Stefan Johnson and Michael Pollack

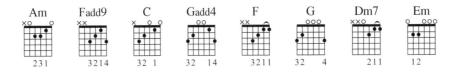

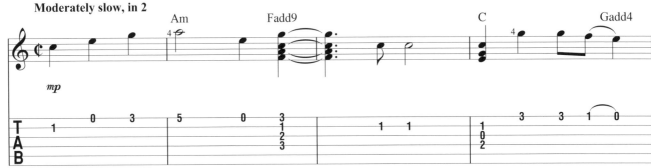

*Capo II

Strum Pattern: 4, 6

Pick Pattern: 4, 6

Intro

Moderately slow, in 2

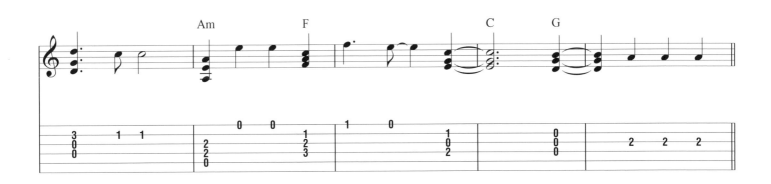

*Optional: To match recording, place capo at 2nd fret

Verse

1. Young blood thinks there's al - ways to - mor - row.
2. Young blood thinks there's al - ways to - mor - row.

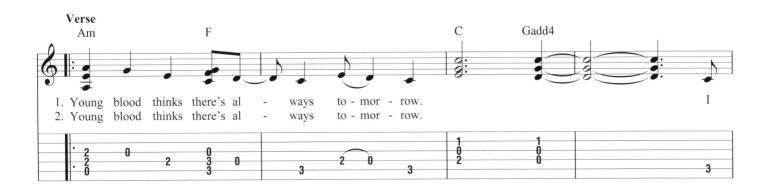

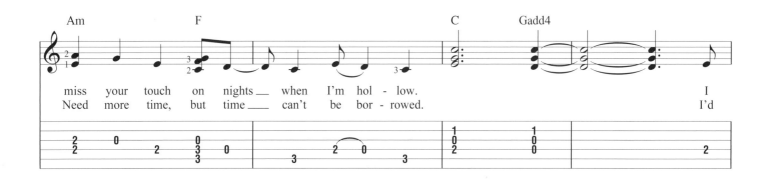

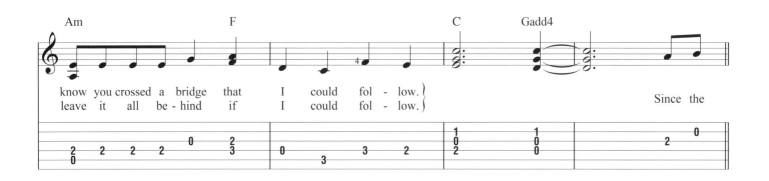

Pre-Chorus

Chorus

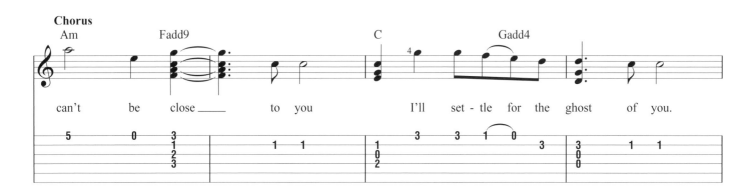

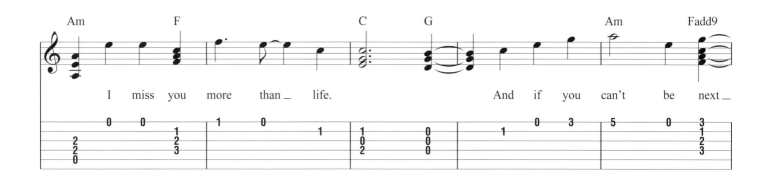

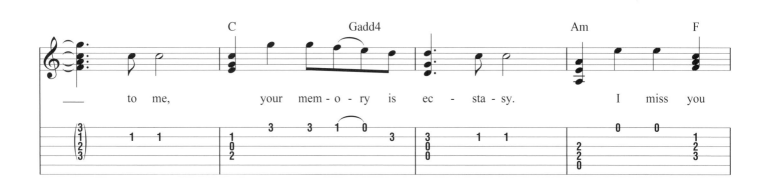

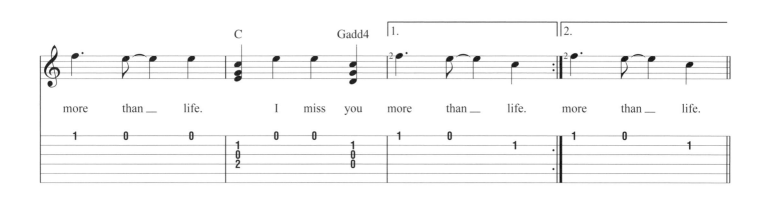

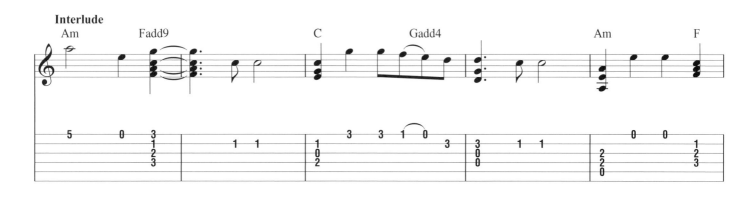

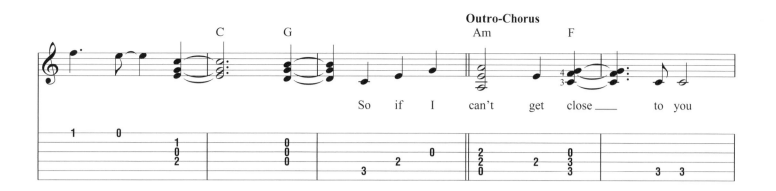

Outro-Chorus

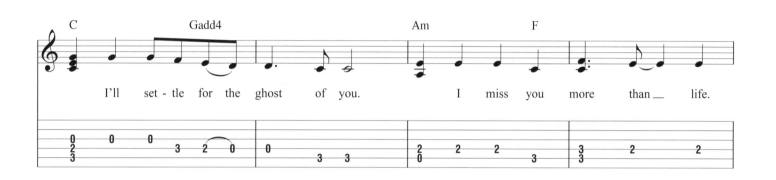

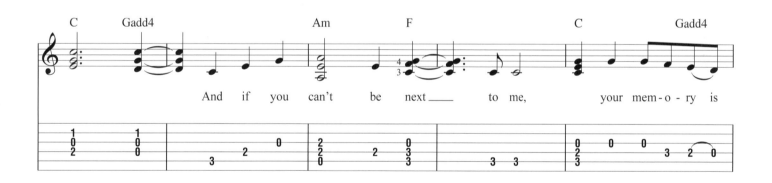

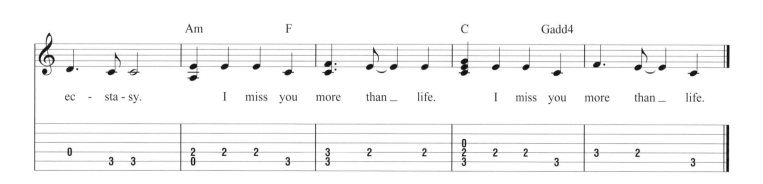

Happier Than Ever

Words and Music by Billie Eilish O'Connell and Finneas O'Connell

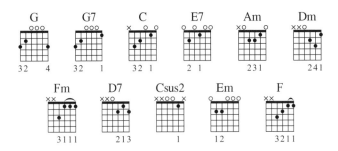

Strum Pattern: 4, 8
Pick Pattern: 3, 8

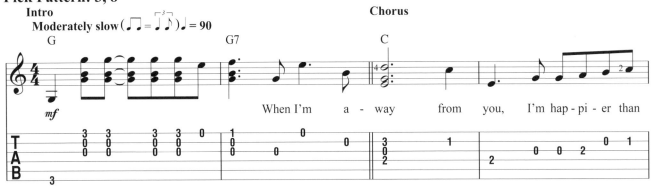

When I'm a - way from you, I'm hap - pi - er than

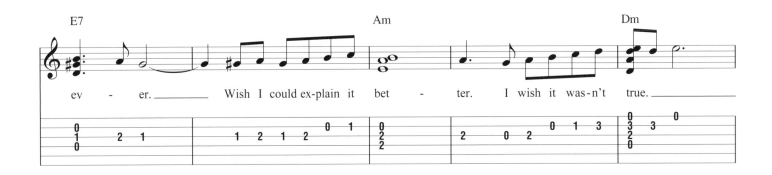

ev - er. ___ Wish I could ex-plain it bet - ter. I wish it was-n't true. ___

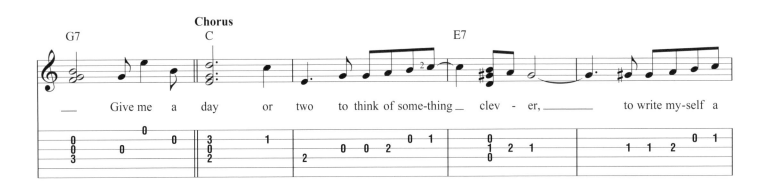

___ Give me a day or two to think of some-thing ___ clev - er, ___ to write my-self a

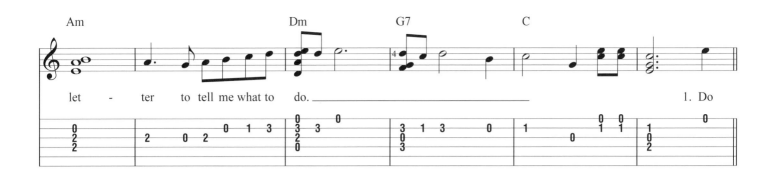

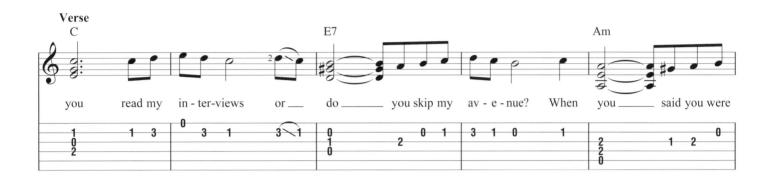

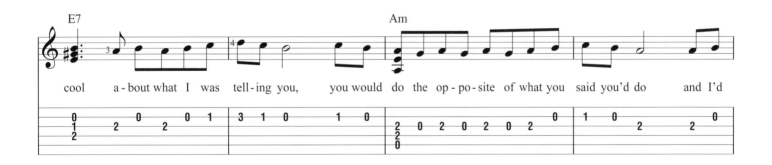

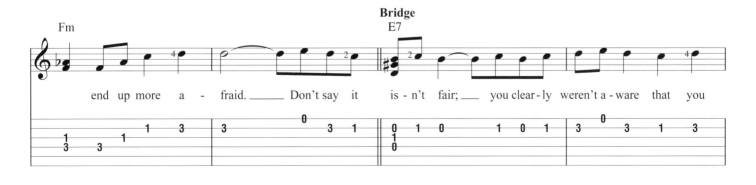

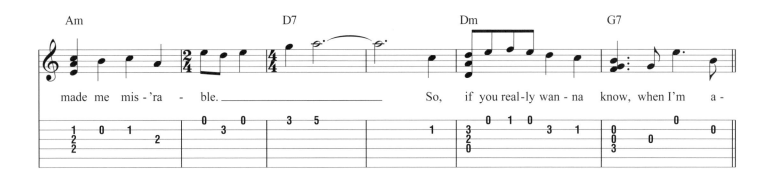

made me mis-'ra-ble. So, if you real-ly wan-na know, when I'm a-

Chorus

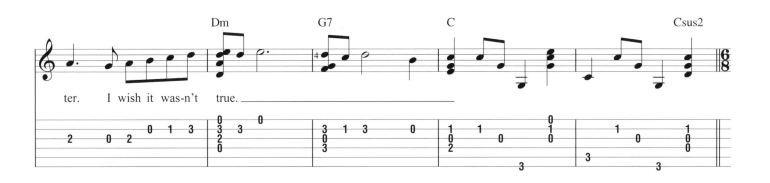

way from you, I'm hap-pi-er than ev - - er._____ Wish I could ex-plain it bet -

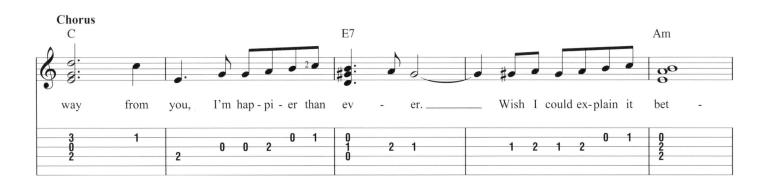

ter. I wish it was-n't true._____

Interlude
Slow, in 2 ♩. = 52

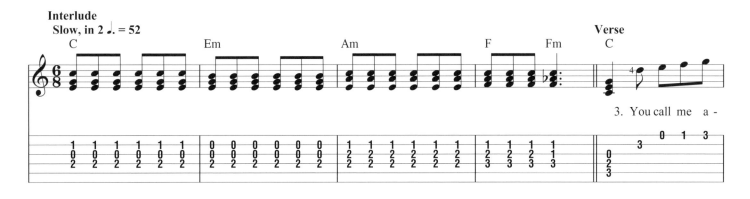

3. You call me a-

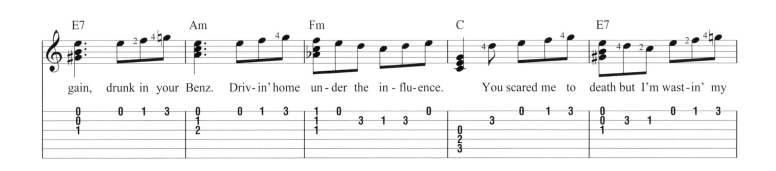

gain, drunk in your Benz. Driv-in' home un-der the in - flu-ence. You scared me to death but I'm wast-in' my

breath 'cause you on - ly lis - ten to your fuck - in' friends. 4. I don't re - late to you. I don't re - late to you,

no. 'Cause I'd nev - er treat me this shit - ty. You made me hate this cit - y. 5. And I don't talk

Verse

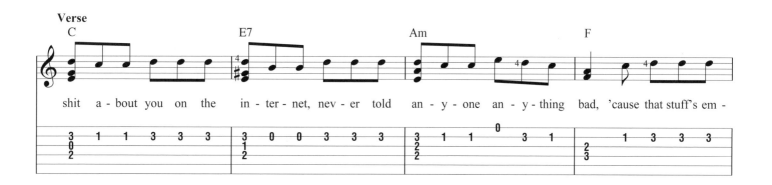

shit a - bout you on the in - ter - net, nev - er told an - y - one an - y - thing bad, 'cause that stuff's em -

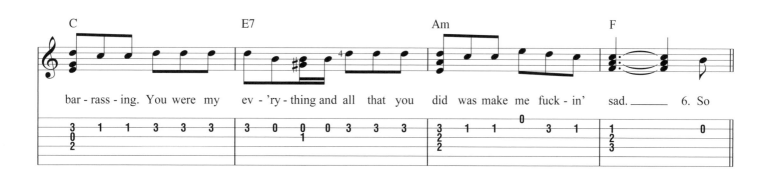

bar - rass - ing. You were my ev - 'ry - thing and all that you did was make me fuck - in' sad. _____ 6. So

Verse

don't waste the time I don't have _____ and don't try to make me feel bad. I could talk a - bout

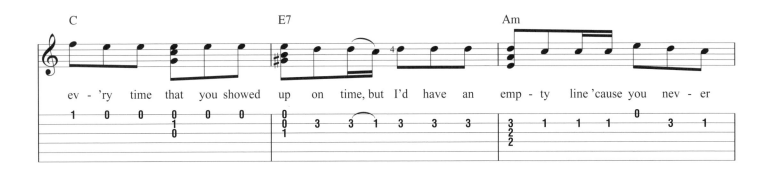

ev - ’ry time that you showed up on time, but I’d have an emp - ty line ’cause you nev - er

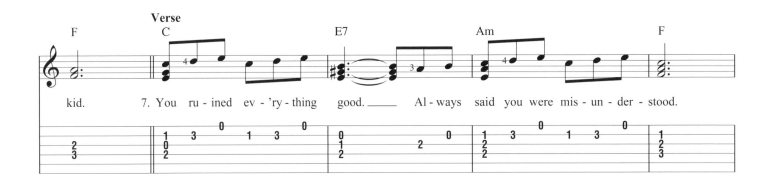

did. Nev - er paid an - y mind to my moth - er or friends, so I shut ’em all out for you ’cause I was a

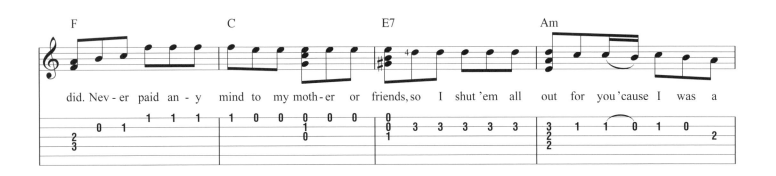

Verse

kid. 7. You ru - ined ev - ’ry - thing good. _____ Al - ways said you were mis - un - der - stood.

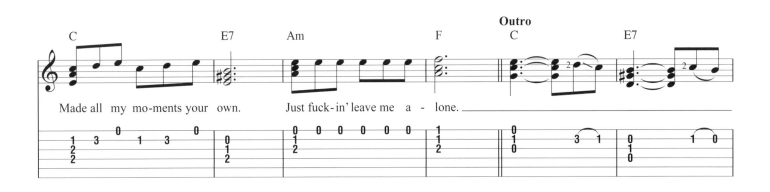

Outro

Made all my mo - ments your own. Just fuck - in’ leave me a - lone. _____

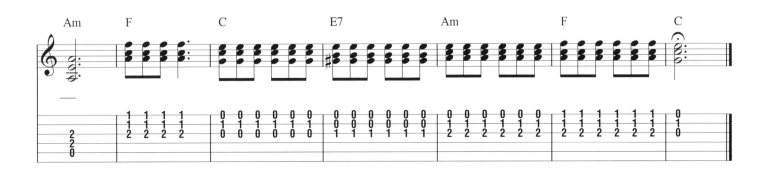

Smokin' Out the Window

Words and Music by Peter Gene Hernandez, Dernst Emile and Anderson .Paak

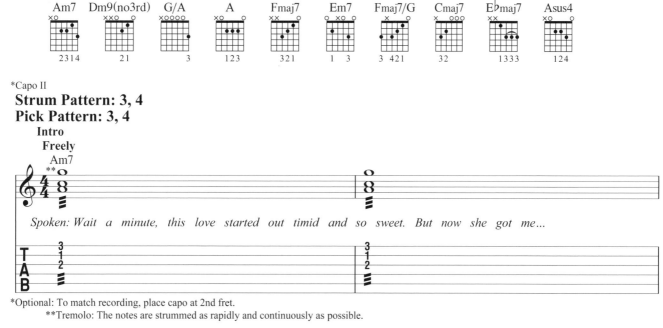

*Capo II

Strum Pattern: 3, 4
Pick Pattern: 3, 4

Intro
Freely

Spoken: Wait a minute, this love started out timid and so sweet. But now she got me...

*Optional: To match recording, place capo at 2nd fret.
**Tremolo: The notes are strummed as rapidly and continuously as possible.

Moderately slow

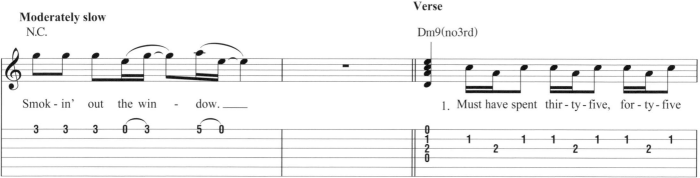

Smok-in' out the win - dow. _____

Verse

1. Must have spent thir-ty-five, for-ty-five

thou-sand up at Tif-fa-ny's. _____ Oh, no! _____ Got her bad - ass kids run-ning 'round my whole

crib like it's Chuck E. Cheese. _____ Whoa, whoa. _____ Put me in a jam with her ex - man in the

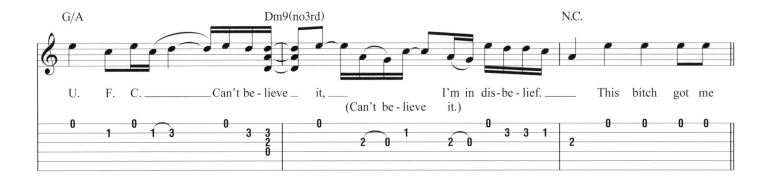

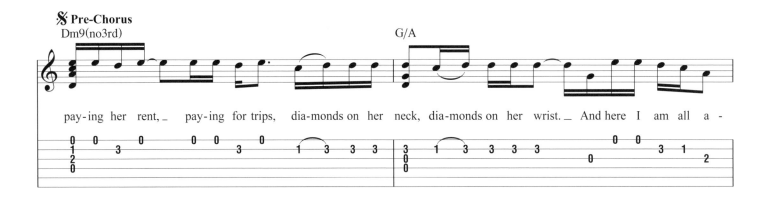

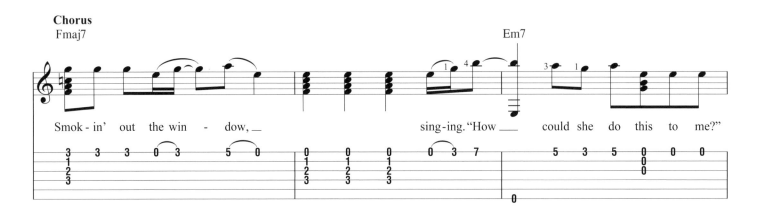

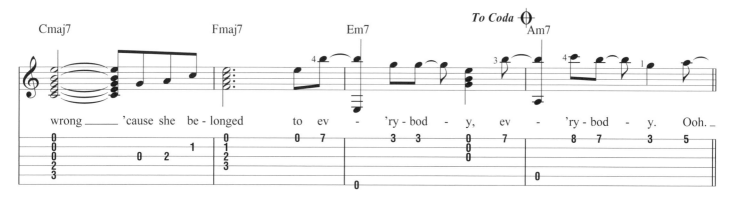

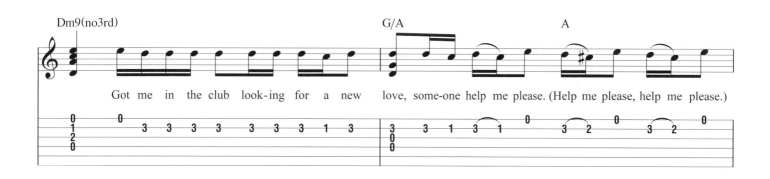

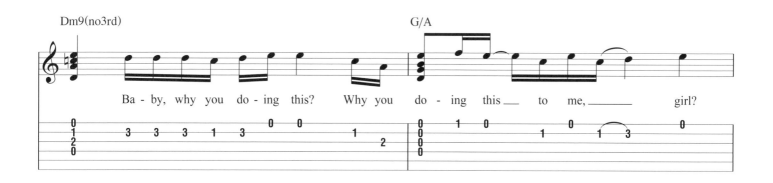

Not to be dra-ma-tic, but I want to die. This bitch got me

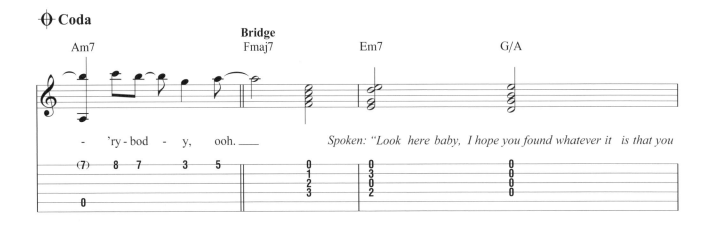

Coda

Bridge

-'ry-bod-y, ooh.

Spoken: "Look here baby, I hope you found whatever it is that you

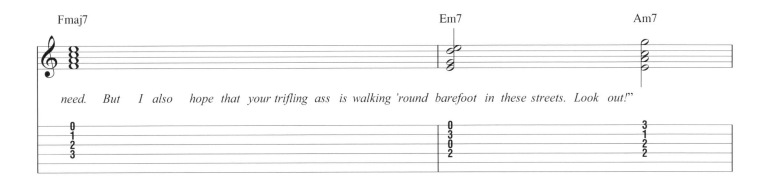

need. But I also hope that your trifling ass is walking 'round barefoot in these streets. Look out!"

Girl, it breaks my heart that you ain't right here with me. Now, I

*Sung one octave higher, next 4 measures

Outro-Chorus

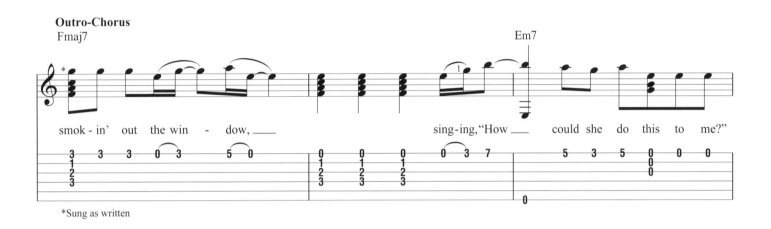

*Sung as written

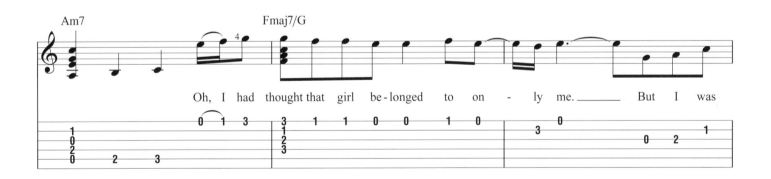

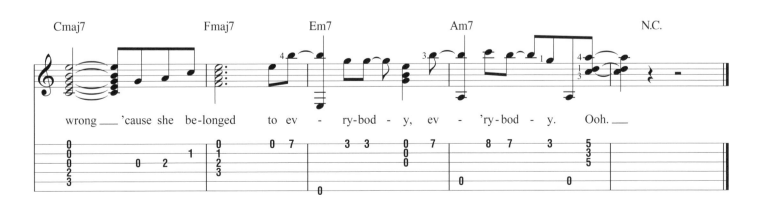

Shivers

Words and Music by Ed Sheeran, Johnny McDaid, Steve Mac and Kal Lavelle

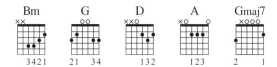

Strum Pattern: 6
Pick Pattern: 4

Intro
Moderately fast

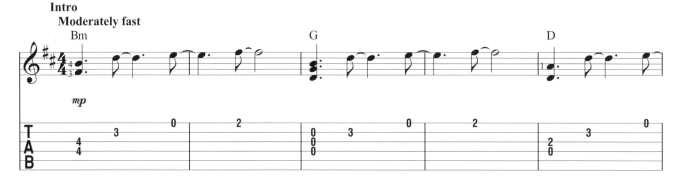

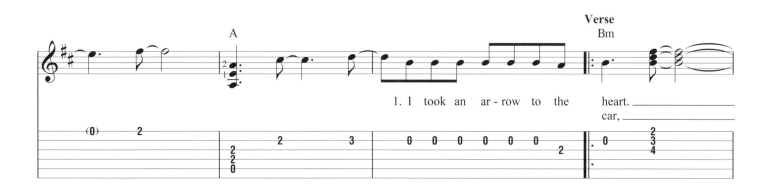

1. I took an ar-row to the heart.
car,

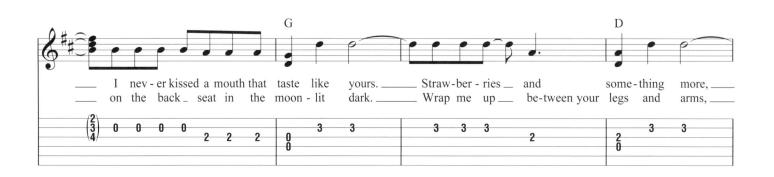

___ I nev-er kissed a mouth that taste like yours. ___ Straw-ber-ries ___ and some-thing more, ___
___ on the back ___ seat in the moon-lit dark. ___ Wrap me up be-tween your legs and arms, ___

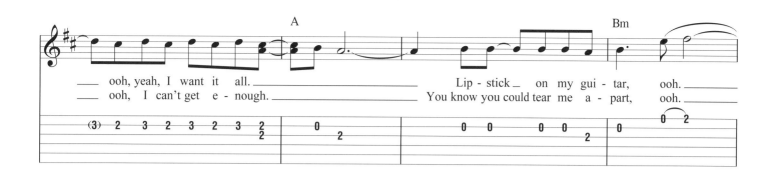

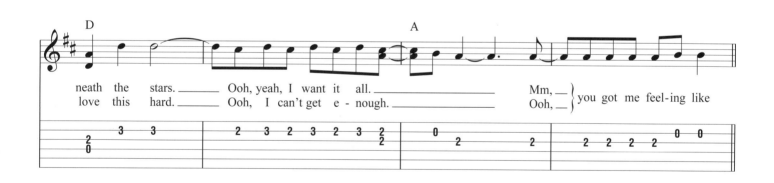

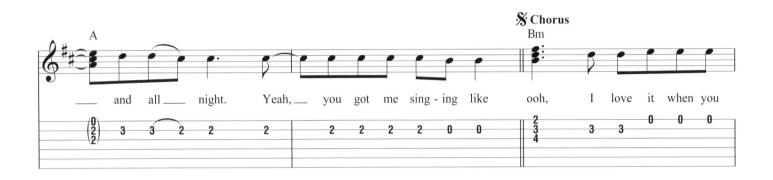

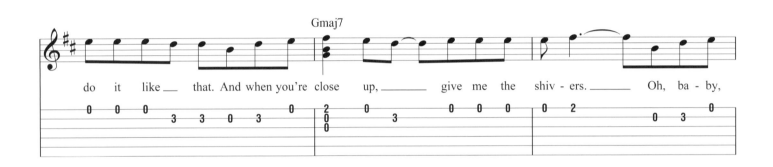

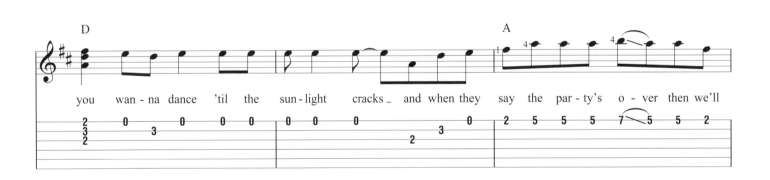

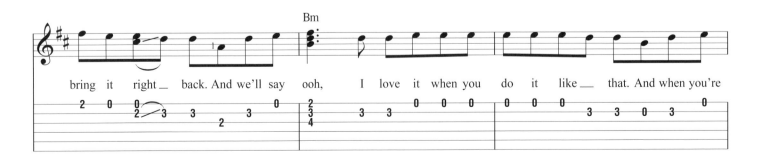

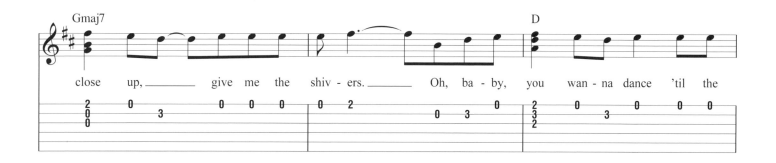

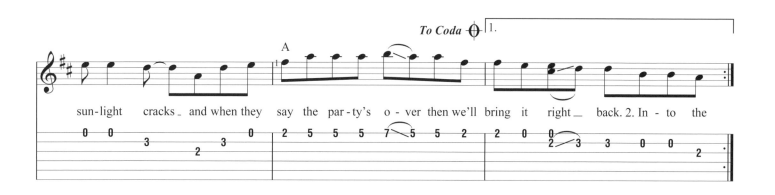

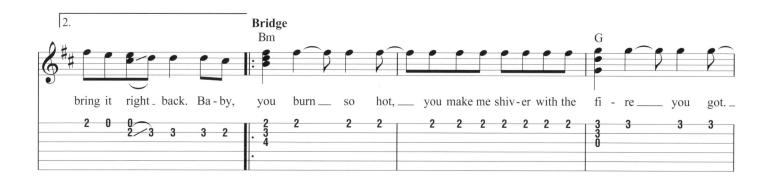

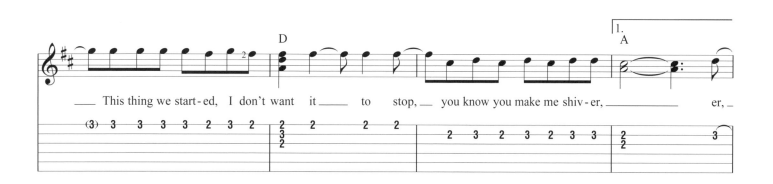

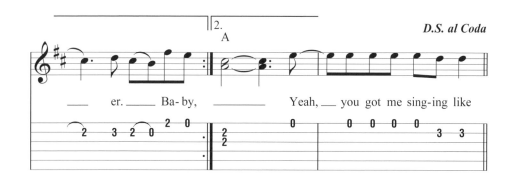

VBS

Words and Music by Lucy Dacus

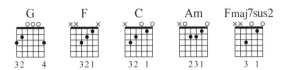

Strum Pattern: 3
Pick Pattern: 3

Verse
Moderately slow

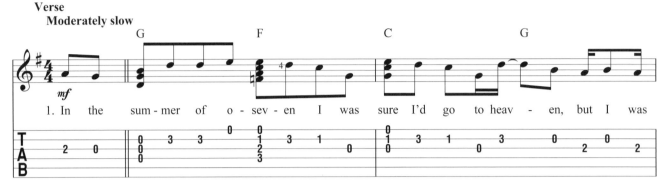

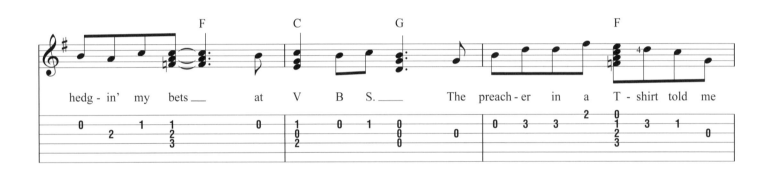

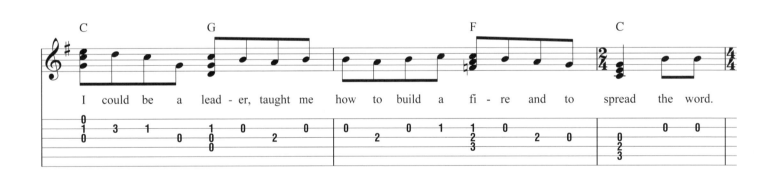

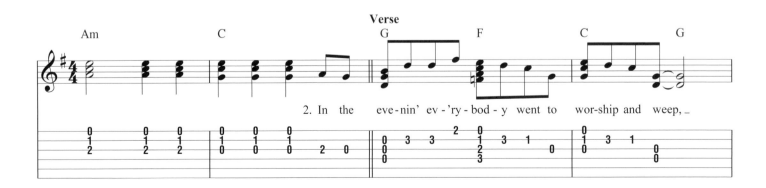

hands a - bove our heads, reach - ing for God. __ Back in the cab - in snort - in'

nut - meg in your bunk bed you were wait - in' for a rev - e - la - tion of your own.

Verse

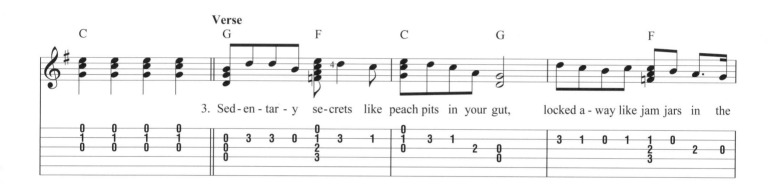

3. Sed - en - tar - y se - crets like peach pits in your gut, locked a - way like jam jars in the

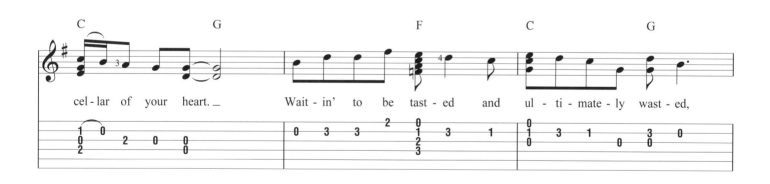

cel - lar of your heart. __ Wait - in' to be tast - ed and ul - ti - mate - ly wast - ed,

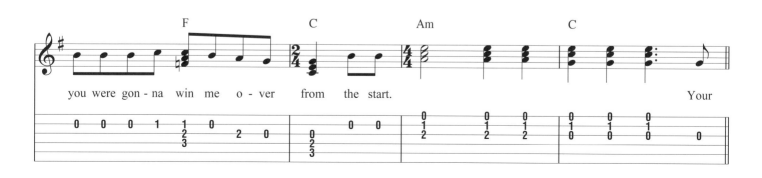

you were gon - na win me o - ver from the start. Your

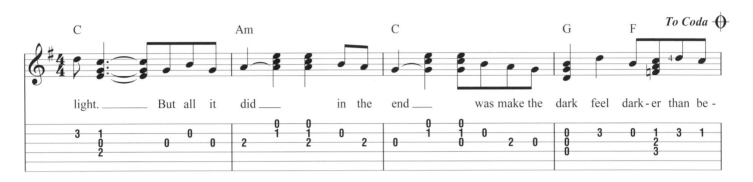

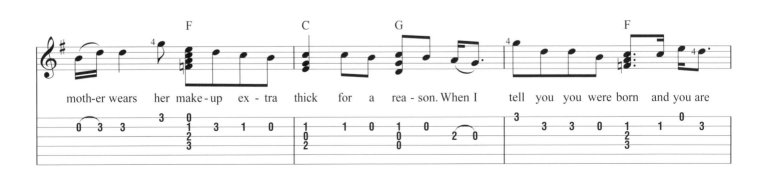

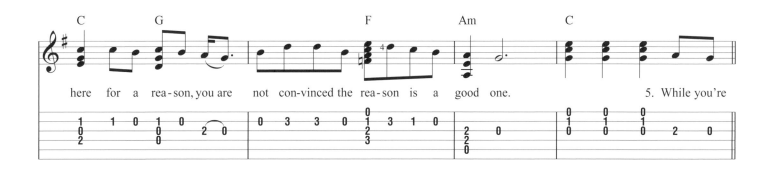

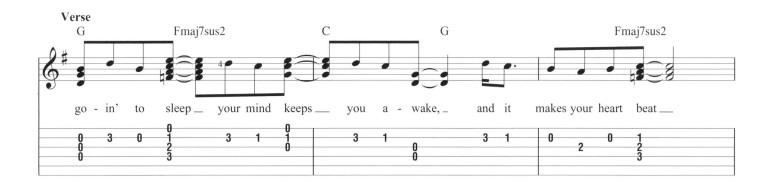

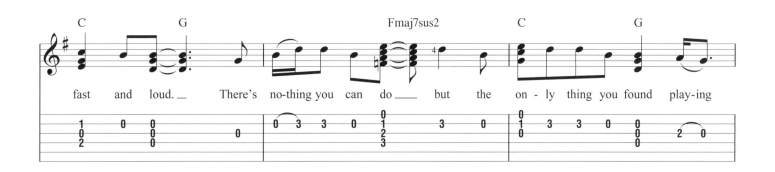

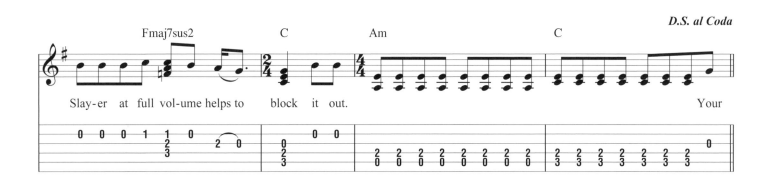

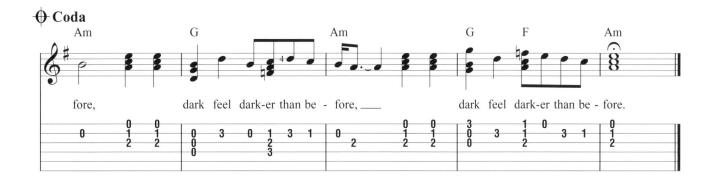

We Don't Talk About Bruno

from ENCANTO

Music and Lyrics by Lin-Manuel Miranda

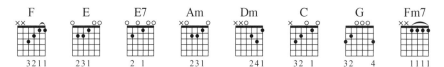

*Capo III

Strum Pattern: 4

Pick Pattern: 4

Intro

Moderately

*Optional: To match recording, place capo at 3rd fret.

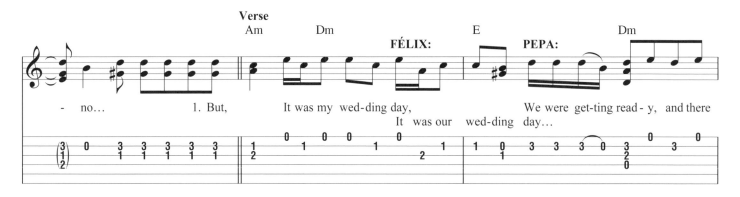

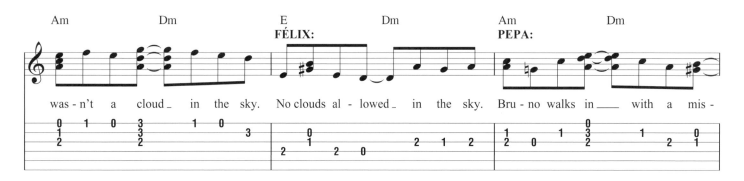

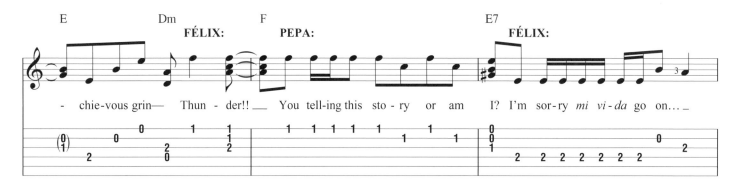

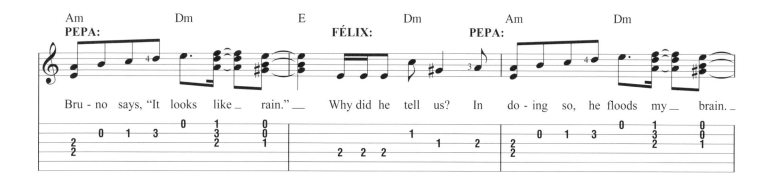

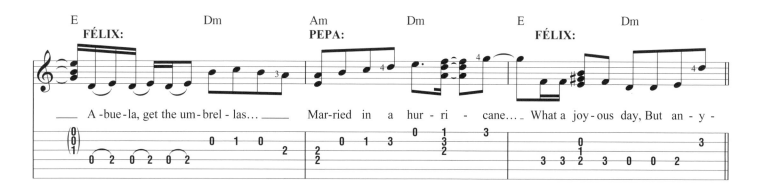

Chorus

Verse

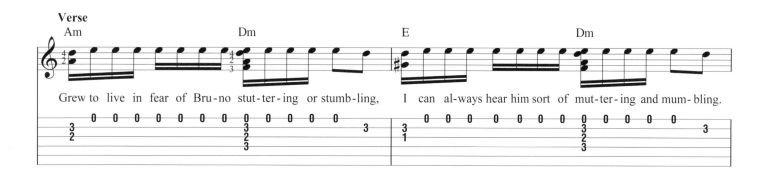

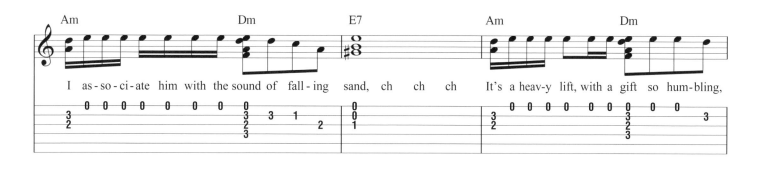

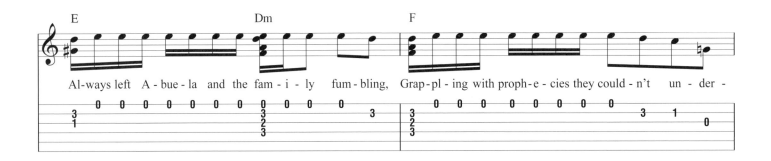

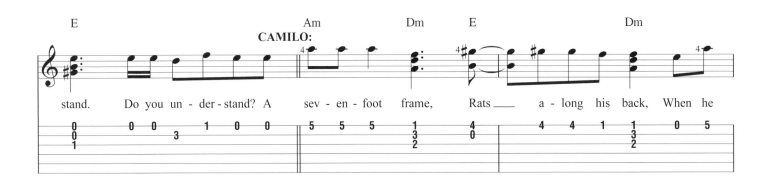

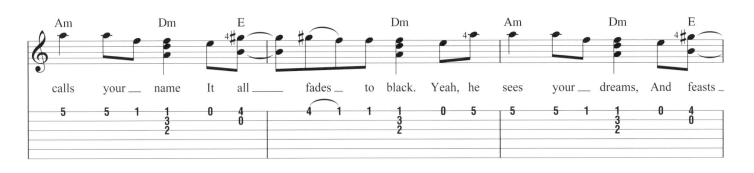

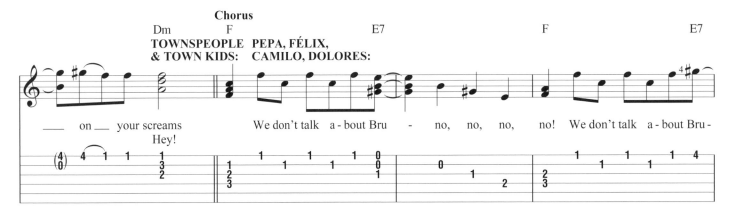

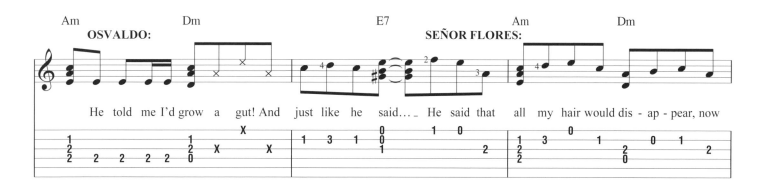

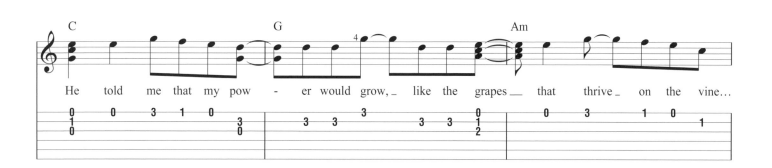

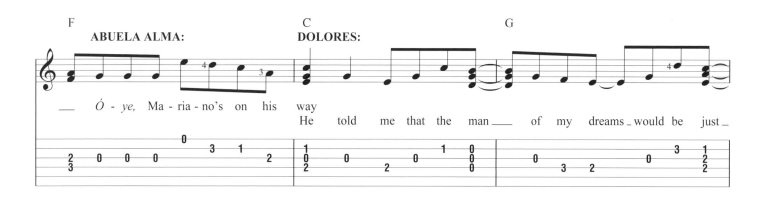

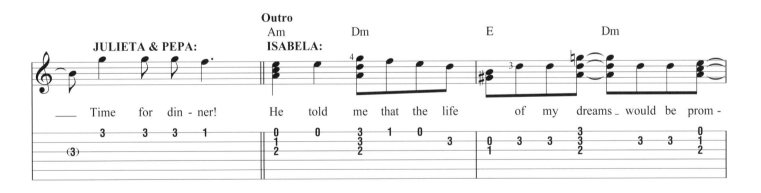

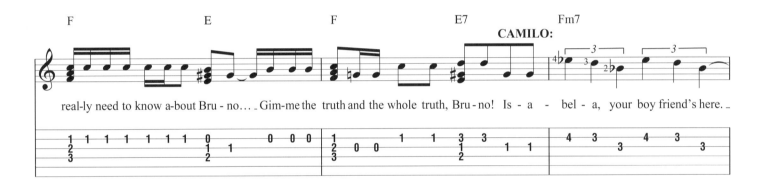

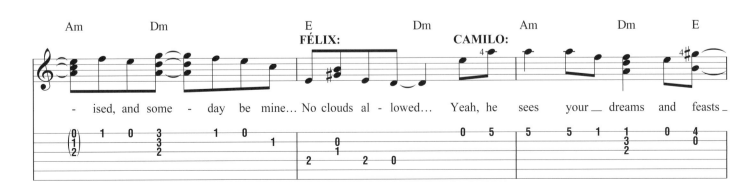

You Should Probably Leave

Words and Music by Chris Stapleton, Chris DuBois and Ashley Gorley

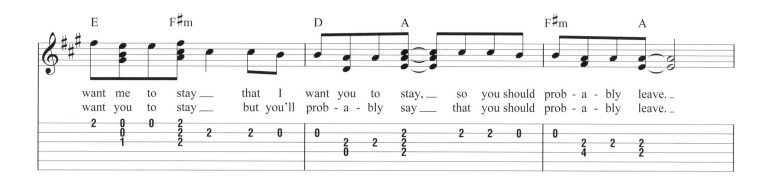

want me to stay ___ that I want you to stay, __ so you should prob - a - bly leave. __
want you to stay __ but you'll prob - a - bly say __ that you should prob - a - bly leave. __

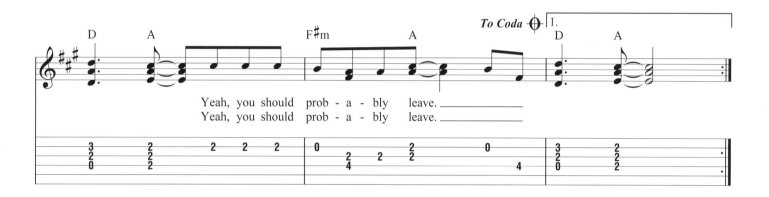

Yeah, you should prob - a - bly leave. _____
Yeah, you should prob - a - bly leave. _____

Like a dev - il on my shoul-der, you keep whis-per-in' in my ear. __

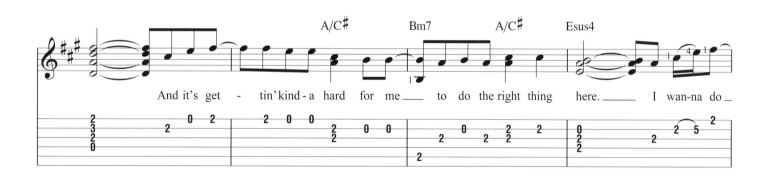

And it's get - tin' kind-a hard for me ___ to do the right thing here. _____ I wan-na do __

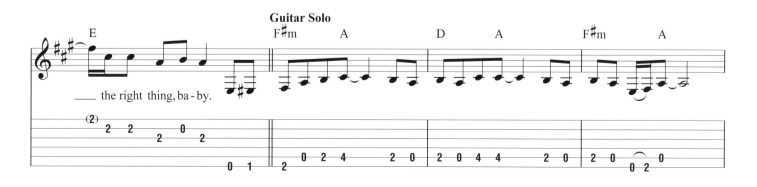

___ the right thing, ba - by.

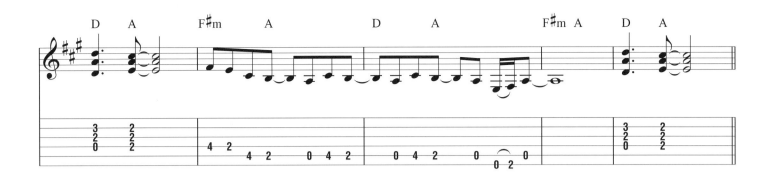

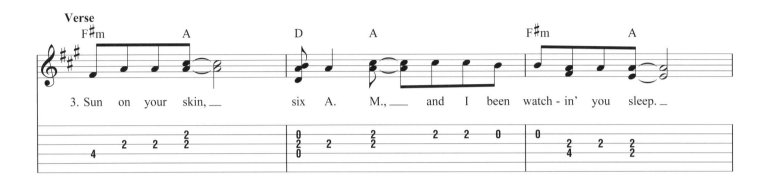

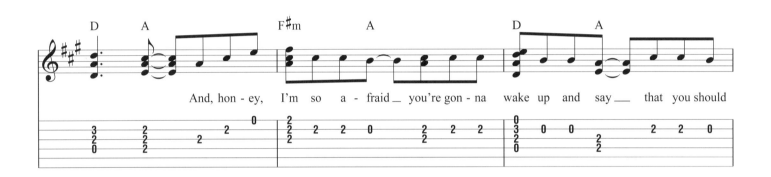

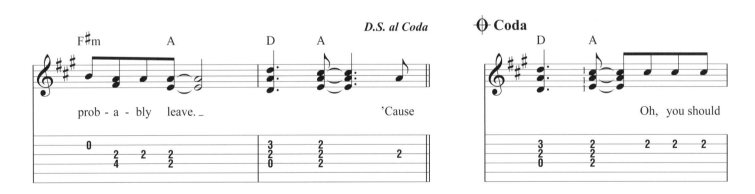

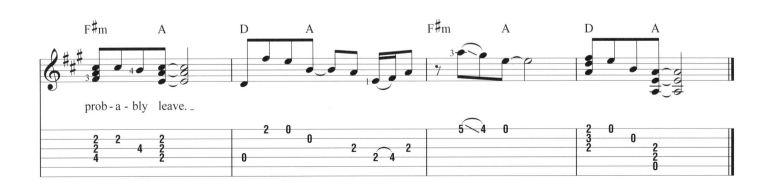

This series features simplified arrangements with notes, tab, chord charts, and strum and pick patterns.

MIXED FOLIOS

00702287	Acoustic	$19.99
00702002	Acoustic Rock Hits for Easy Guitar	$15.99
00702166	All-Time Best Guitar Collection	$19.99
00702232	Best Acoustic Songs for Easy Guitar	$16.99
00119835	Best Children's Songs	$16.99
00703055	The Big Book of Nursery Rhymes & Children's Songs	$16.99
00698978	Big Christmas Collection	$19.99
00702394	Bluegrass Songs for Easy Guitar	$15.99
00289632	Bohemian Rhapsody	$19.99
00703387	Celtic Classics	$14.99
00224808	Chart Hits of 2016-2017	$14.99
00267383	Chart Hits of 2017-2018	$14.99
00334293	Chart Hits of 2019-2020	$16.99
00702149	Children's Christian Songbook	$9.99
00702028	Christmas Classics	$8.99
00101779	Christmas Guitar	$14.99
00702141	Classic Rock	$8.95
00159642	Classical Melodies	$12.99
00253933	Disney/Pixar's Coco	$16.99
00702203	CMT's 100 Greatest Country Songs	$34.99
00702283	The Contemporary Christian Collection	$16.99
00196954	Contemporary Disney	$19.99
00702239	Country Classics for Easy Guitar	$24.99

00702257	Easy Acoustic Guitar Songs	$16.99
00702041	Favorite Hymns for Easy Guitar	$12.99
00222701	Folk Pop Songs	$17.99
00126894	Frozen	$14.99
00333922	Frozen 2	$14.99
00702286	Glee	$16.99
00702160	The Great American Country Songbook	$19.99
00702148	Great American Gospel for Guitar	$14.99
00702050	Great Classical Themes for Easy Guitar	$9.99
00275088	The Greatest Showman	$17.99
00148030	Halloween Guitar Songs	$14.99
00702273	Irish Songs	$12.99
00192503	Jazz Classics for Easy Guitar	$16.99
00702275	Jazz Favorites for Easy Guitar	$17.99
00702274	Jazz Standards for Easy Guitar	$19.99
00702162	Jumbo Easy Guitar Songbook	$24.99
00232285	La La Land	$16.99
00702258	Legends of Rock	$14.99
00702189	MTV's 100 Greatest Pop Songs	$34.99
00702272	1950s Rock	$16.99
00702271	1960s Rock	$16.99
00702270	1970s Rock	$19.99
00702269	1980s Rock	$15.99
00702268	1990s Rock	$19.99
00369043	Rock Songs for Kids	$14.99

00109725	Once	$14.99
00702187	Selections from O Brother Where Art Thou?	$19.99
00702178	100 Songs for Kids	$14.99
00702515	Pirates of the Caribbean	$17.99
00702125	Praise and Worship for Guitar	$14.99
00287930	Songs from *A Star Is Born, The Greatest Showman, La La Land,* and More Movie Musicals	$16.99
00702285	Southern Rock Hits	$12.99
00156420	Star Wars Music	$16.99
00121535	30 Easy Celtic Guitar Solos	$16.99
00702156	3-Chord Rock	$12.99
00244654	Top Hits of 2017	$14.99
00283786	Top Hits of 2018	$14.99
00702294	Top Worship Hits	$17.99
00702255	VH1's 100 Greatest Hard Rock Songs	$34.99
00702175	VH1's 100 Greatest Songs of Rock and Roll	$29.99
00702253	Wicked	$12.99

ARTIST COLLECTIONS

00702267	AC/DC for Easy Guitar	$16.99
00702598	Adele for Easy Guitar	$15.99
00156221	Adele – 25	$16.99
00702040	Best of the Allman Brothers	$16.99
00702865	J.S. Bach for Easy Guitar	$15.99
00702169	Best of The Beach Boys	$15.99
00702292	The Beatles — 1	$22.99
00125796	Best of Chuck Berry	$15.99
00702201	The Essential Black Sabbath	$15.99
00702250	blink-182 — Greatest Hits	$17.99
02501615	Zac Brown Band — The Foundation	$17.99
02501621	Zac Brown Band — You Get What You Give	$16.99
00702043	Best of Johnny Cash	$17.99
00702090	Eric Clapton's Best	$16.99
00702086	Eric Clapton — from the Album Unplugged	$17.99
00702202	The Essential Eric Clapton	$17.99
00702053	Best of Patsy Cline	$15.99
00222697	Very Best of Coldplay – 2nd Edition	$16.99
00702229	The Very Best of Creedence Clearwater Revival	$16.99
00702145	Best of Jim Croce	$16.99
00702278	Crosby, Stills & Nash	$12.99
14042809	Bob Dylan	$15.99
00702276	Fleetwood Mac — Easy Guitar Collection	$17.99
00139462	The Very Best of Grateful Dead	$16.99
00702136	Best of Merle Haggard	$16.99
00702227	Jimi Hendrix — Smash Hits	$19.99
00702288	Best of Hillsong United	$12.99
00702236	Best of Antonio Carlos Jobim	$15.99
00702245	Elton John — Greatest Hits 1970–2002	$19.99

00129855	Jack Johnson	$16.99
00702204	Robert Johnson	$14.99
00702234	Selections from Toby Keith — 35 Biggest Hits	$12.95
00702003	Kiss	$16.99
00702216	Lynyrd Skynyrd	$16.99
00702182	The Essential Bob Marley	$16.99
00146081	Maroon 5	$14.99
00121925	Bruno Mars – Unorthodox Jukebox	$12.99
00702248	Paul McCartney — All the Best	$14.99
00125484	The Best of MercyMe	$12.99
00702209	Steve Miller Band — Young Hearts (Greatest Hits)	$12.95
00124167	Jason Mraz	$15.99
00702096	Best of Nirvana	$16.99
00702211	The Offspring — Greatest Hits	$17.99
00138026	One Direction	$17.99
00702030	Best of Roy Orbison	$17.99
00702144	Best of Ozzy Osbourne	$14.99
00702279	Tom Petty	$17.99
00102911	Pink Floyd	$17.99
00702139	Elvis Country Favorites	$19.99
00702293	The Very Best of Prince	$19.99
00699415	Best of Queen for Guitar	$16.99
00109279	Best of R.E.M.	$14.99
00702208	Red Hot Chili Peppers — Greatest Hits	$16.99
00198960	The Rolling Stones	$17.99
00174793	The Very Best of Santana	$16.99
00702196	Best of Bob Seger	$16.99
00146046	Ed Sheeran	$15.99
00702252	Frank Sinatra — Nothing But the Best	$12.99
00702010	Best of Rod Stewart	$17.99
00702049	Best of George Strait	$17.99

00702259	Taylor Swift for Easy Guitar	$15.99
00359800	Taylor Swift – Easy Guitar Anthology	$24.99
00702260	Taylor Swift — Fearless	$14.99
00139727	Taylor Swift — 1989	$17.99
00115960	Taylor Swift — Red	$16.99
00253667	Taylor Swift — Reputation	$17.99
00702290	Taylor Swift — Speak Now	$16.99
00232849	Chris Tomlin Collection – 2nd Edition	$14.99
00702226	Chris Tomlin — See the Morning	$12.95
00148643	Train	$14.99
00702427	U2 — 18 Singles	$19.99
00702108	Best of Stevie Ray Vaughan	$17.99
00279005	The Who	$14.99
00702123	Best of Hank Williams	$15.99
00194548	Best of John Williams	$14.99
00702228	Neil Young — Greatest Hits	$17.99
00119133	Neil Young — Harvest	$14.99

Prices, contents and availability subject to change without notice.

HAL•LEONARD®

Visit Hal Leonard online at **halleonard.com**

Get Better at Guitar
...with these Great Guitar Instruction Books from Hal Leonard!

101 GUITAR TIPS
INCLUDES TAB
STUFF ALL THE PROS KNOW AND USE
by Adam St. James
This book contains invaluable guidance on everything from scales and music theory to truss rod adjustments, proper recording studio set-ups, and much more.

00695737 Book/Online Audio $17.99

AMAZING PHRASING
INCLUDES TAB
by Tom Kolb
This book/audio pack explores all the main components necessary for crafting well-balanced rhythmic and melodic phrases. It also explains how these phrases are put together to form cohesive solos. The companion audio contains 89 demo tracks, most with full-band backing.

00695583 Book/Online Audio $22.99

ARPEGGIOS FOR THE MODERN GUITARIST
INCLUDES TAB
by Tom Kolb
Using this no-nonsense book with online audio, guitarists will learn to apply and execute all types of arpeggio forms using a variety of techniques, including alternate picking, sweep picking, tapping, string skipping, and legato.

00695862 Book/Online Audio $22.99

BLUES YOU CAN USE
by John Ganapes
This comprehensive source for learning blues guitar is designed to develop both your lead and rhythm playing. Includes: 21 complete solos • blues chords, progressions and riffs • turnarounds • movable scales and soloing techniques • string bending • utilizing the entire fingerboard • and more.

00142420 Book/Online Media................................$22.99

CONNECTING PENTATONIC PATTERNS
INCLUDES TAB
by Tom Kolb
If you've been finding yourself trapped in the pentatonic box, this book is for you! This hands-on book with online audio offers examples for guitar players of all levels, from beginner to advanced. Study this book faithfully, and soon you'll be soloing all over the neck with the greatest of ease.

00696445 Book/Online Audio $24.99

FRETBOARD MASTERY
INCLUDES TAB
by Troy Stetina
Untangle the mysterious regions of the guitar fretboard and unlock your potential. This book familiarizes you with all the shapes you need to know by applying them in real musical examples, thereby reinforcing and reaffirming your newfound knowledge.

00695331 Book/Online Audio $22.99

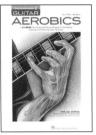

GUITAR AEROBICS
INCLUDES TAB
by Troy Nelson
Here is a daily dose of guitar "vitamins" to keep your chops fine tuned! Musical styles include rock, blues, jazz, metal, country, and funk. Techniques taught include alternate picking, arpeggios, sweep picking, string skipping, legato, string bending, and rhythm guitar.

00695946 Book/Online Audio $24.99

GUITAR CLUES
INCLUDES TAB
OPERATION PENTATONIC
by Greg Koch
Whether you're new to improvising or have been doing it for a while, this book/audio pack will provide loads of delicious licks and tricks that you can use right away, from volume swells and chicken pickin' to intervallic and chordal ideas.

00695827 Book/Online Audio $19.99

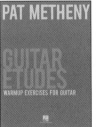

PAT METHENY – GUITAR ETUDES
INCLUDES TAB
Over the years, in many master classes and workshops around the world, Pat has demonstrated the kind of daily workout he puts himself through. This book includes a collection of 14 guitar etudes he created to help you limber up, improve picking technique and build finger independence.

00696587..$17.99

PICTURE CHORD ENCYCLOPEDIA
This comprehensive guitar chord resource for all playing styles and levels features five voicings of 44 chord qualities for all twelve keys – 2,640 chords in all! For each, there is a clearly illustrated chord frame, as well as *an actual photo* of the chord being played!.

00695224..$22.99

RHYTHM GUITAR 365
INCLUDES TAB
by Troy Nelson
This book provides 365 exercises – one for every day of the year! – to keep your rhythm chops fine tuned. Topics covered include: chord theory; the fundamentals of rhythm; fingerpicking; strum patterns; diatonic and non-diatonic progressions; triads; major and minor keys; and more.

00103627 Book/Online Audio $27.99

SCALE CHORD RELATIONSHIPS
INCLUDES TAB
by Michael Mueller & Jeff Schroedl
This book/audio pack explains how to: recognize keys • analyze chord progressions • use the modes • play over nondiatonic harmony • use harmonic and melodic minor scales • use symmetrical scales • incorporate exotic scales • and much more!

00695563 Book/Online Audio $17.99

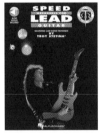

SPEED MECHANICS FOR LEAD GUITAR
INCLUDES TAB
by Troy Stetina
Take your playing to the stratosphere with this advanced lead book which will help you develop speed and precision in today's explosive playing styles. Learn the fastest ways to achieve speed and control, secrets to make your practice time really count, and how to open your ears and make your musical ideas more solid and tangible.

00699323 Book/Online Audio $22.99

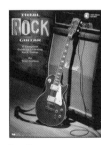

TOTAL ROCK GUITAR
INCLUDES TAB
by Troy Stetina
This comprehensive source for learning rock guitar is designed to develop both lead and rhythm playing. It covers: getting a tone that rocks • open chords, power chords and barre chords • riffs, scales and licks • string bending, strumming, and harmonics • and more.

00695246 Book/Online Audio $22.99

Guitar World Presents STEVE VAI'S GUITAR WORKOUT
INCLUDES TAB
In this book, Steve Vai reveals his path to virtuoso enlightenment with two challenging guitar workouts – one 10-hour and one 30-hour – which include scale and chord exercises, ear training, sight-reading, music theory, and much more.

00119643..$16.99

HAL•LEONARD®

Prices, contents, and availability subject to change without notice.

Order these and more publications from your favorite music retailer at
halleonard.com

0322
032